Arguments for revolutionary socialism

ARGUMENTS FOR REVOLUTIONARY SOCIALISM

JOHN MOLYNEUX

Bookmarks
London, Chicago and Melbourne

Arguments for Revolutionary Socialism
by John Molyneux

Published April 1987
Bookmarks, 265 Seven Sisters Road, London N4 2DE, England.
Bookmarks, PO Box 16085, Chicago, IL 60616, USA.
Bookmarks, GPO Box 1473N, Melbourne 3001, Australia.

ISBN 0 906224 35 7

Printed by Cox and Wyman Limited, Reading, England.
Typeset by Kate Macpherson, Clevedon, Avon.
Design by Roger Huddle.

BOOKMARKS is linked to an international grouping of socialist organisations:

AUSTRALIA: **International Socialists**, GPO Box 1473N, Melbourne 3001.
BELGIUM: **Socialisme International**, 9 rue Marexhe, 4400 Herstal, Liege.
BRITAIN: **Socialist Workers Party**, PO Box 82, London E3.
CANADA: **International Socialists**, PO Box 339, Station E, Toronto, Ontario.
DENMARK: **Internationale Socialister**, Morten Borupsgade 18, kld, 8000 Arhus C.
FRANCE: **Socialisme International** (correspondence to Yves Coleman, BP 407, Paris Cedex 05).
IRELAND: **Socialist Workers Movement**, PO Box 1648, Dublin 8.
NORWAY: **Internasjonale Sosialister**, Postboks 5370, Majorstua, 0304 Oslo 3.
UNITED STATES: **International Socialist Organization**, PO Box 16085, Chicago, Illinois 60616.
WEST GERMANY: **Sozialistische Arbeiter Gruppe**, Wolfgangstrasse 81, D-6000 Frankfurt 1.

This book is published with the aid of the
Bookmarks Publishing Co-operative.
Many socialists have a few savings put
aside, probably in a bank or savings bank.
While it's there, this money is being
re-loaned by the bank to some business or
other to further the aims of capitalism.
We believe it is better loaned to a socialist
venture to further the struggle for
socialism. That's how the co-operative
works: in return for a loan, repayable at a
month's notice, members receive free
copies of books published by Bookmarks,
plus other advantages. The co-operative
has about 130 members at the time this
book is published, from as far apart as
London and Australia, Canada and
Norway.

Like to know more? Write to the
Bookmarks Publishing Co-operative,
265 Seven Sisters Road, London N4 2DE,
England.

Contents

FOREWORD / 9

WHAT DO YOU MEAN BY SOCIALISM? / 13

'But you can't change human nature . . .'
Won't we always need bosses?
Don't revolutions mean violence?
'Under socialism they'd make us all the same . . .'

SO HOW DO WE GET TO THIS NEW WORLD? / 27

Why we don't like Mondays
What do you mean by exploitation?
What is 'capital'?
How capitalism causes crises
Where is history leading?
Socialism or barbarism?
What puts socialist revolution on the agenda?
What we mean by workers' power

GETTING OUR IDEAS RIGHT / 47

'But socialists are such a tiny minority . . .'
Dialectical materialism? What on earth does that mean?
Their truth, and ours
The point, however, is to change it

STRATEGIES OF THE SYSTEM / 57

'You socialists would abolish democracy . . .'
Isn't the state neutral?

Whose law and whose order?
So how do they maintain their rule?
Divided we fall . . .

WHAT DO SOCIALISTS SAY ABOUT . . . ? / 71

Overpopulation
Religion
War
Terrorism
Class
Crime
The family

THE SHAPE OF THE WORLD / 89

Surely we must defend the national interest?
What about immigration?
So do socialists oppose national liberation movements?
What do you mean by 'unconditional but critical' support?
What happened in Russia?
Is China any different?
But isn't a simultaneous world revolution impossible?

STRATEGIES FOR SOCIALISM / 105

'But we've already got a mass workers' party . . . '
Can the Labour Party be changed?
Couldn't we do without organisation?
Do trade unions have a role to play?
What about nationalisation?
What we mean by revolutionary leadership
Many campaigns — only one war
Why we need a revolutionary party

SUGGESTED READING / 125

Foreword

THIS SMALL book is made up from a selection of articles from the 'Teach yourself Marxism' column in **Socialist Worker**, the weekly paper of the Socialist Workers Party. The original articles were written in the years 1983-86 and are reprinted here without significant alteration. They have, however, been selected, grouped under topics and put as far as possible into a coherent order by Steve Wright and Peter Marsden, to whom thanks are due. Inevitably, given the conditions of production, there is a certain amount of overlap and repetition.

The 'Teach yourself Marxism' column is written with two sorts of people particularly in mind. The first is the thinking worker who is beginning to question his or her situation under capitalism, and who wants to find out about socialism and Marxism to see whether they offer a credible alternative. This reader has a multitude of questions arising from their experience, the media, what they were told at school, discussions at work, and so on. The column attempts to answer these questions in as simple and straightforward a way as possible.

The second kind of reader is already a committed and active revolutionary socialist. To be a revolutionary activist is to be a permanent persuader; someone who at work, at union meetings and political meetings, on picket lines and in the pub gets involved in discussion and debate on everything from the latest strike to the role of US imperialism or what went wrong in Russia. In all these discussions the revolutionary socialist has to strive to counter the capitalist system of ideas that dominates most people's thinking, and to put across the socialist, Marxist, point of view. The column aims to assist in this, to provide, again as straightforwardly as possible, some of the arguments the activist needs to have at his or her fingertips.

Not surprisingly, **Arguments for Revolutionary Socialism** has similar audiences in view and similar purposes. In addition, this book hopes to provide an introduction to most of the main ideas of Marxist theory. It is worth pointing out that virtually every argument put forward in these pages is a compressed version of a longer, more developed and substantiated case to be found elsewhere. For example the section on exploitation in chapter two is a condensation of the theory of surplus value to be found in Marx's **Capital** — or more accessibly in his pamphlet **Wage Labour and Capital**, while the Marxist view of terrorism outlined in chapter five is stated more fully in Leon Trotsky's **Against Individual Terrorism**. The interested reader is strongly urged to follow up as many such leads as possible — see our 'Suggested Reading' list at the end of the book.

As an introduction to Marxism this work is one of many; it cannot claim any special merit except, perhaps, one. The majority of commentaries on Marxism treat it as a more or less interesting academic interpretation of the world. This was not at all what its founder intended. Marx produced Marxism not for the university professor and the lecture hall, but for the worker and the factory floor. It is there, a system of ideas for use in all the discussions and battles, large and small, whose sum total constitutes the struggle of the working class for freedom and socialism. Hopefully, **Arguments for Revolutionary Socialism** makes this, at least, clear.

Finally I would like to dedicate this work to Kevin Murphy, a fine friend and comrade over fifteen years and one of the best arguers for revolutionary socialism I know.

John Molyneux
February 1987

Dedication
Albert Holley 1912-1986

Bookmarks would like to dedicate this book to Albert Holley, who joined the International Socialists in the early 1970s and remained an activist in the British Socialist Workers Party right up to his death. Albert was always learning: he was for his class, for socialist revolution, and for internationalism. His whole life was an argument for socialism.

John Molyneux is a member of the Socialist Workers Party in Britain and a regular columnist for the weekly *Socialist Worker*. He is the author of *Marxism and the Party* (1978), *Trotsky's Theory of Revolution* (1981), and *What is the real Marxist tradition?* (1985).

Chapter One:
What do you mean by socialism?

MOST PEOPLE'S ideas of what socialism would be like are dominated by the Stalinist tyranny in Russia or the experiences of Labour or other 'left-wing' governments. That is, they view socialism as either the control of all social life by a bureaucratic and oppressive state or as the status quo modified by a few reforms and somewhat more state intervention.

In the face of these uninspiring alternatives it is tempting to embark on a detailed account of how life would be organised in a genuinely socialist society. In fact Marxists, beginning with Marx himself, have resisted the temptation to draw up a blueprint for socialism as pointless and misleading. If the future society is to be truly socialist, then its details can be decided only by the workers who build it.

Consequently, Marxists have limited themselves to the statement of certain general principles which could be scientifically derived from the study of trends and forces at work under capitalism. These principles clearly differentiate the Marxist conception of socialism from its Stalinist and reformist corruptions.

For Marxists, the fundamental aim of socialism is the creation of a classless society. This is not a single act but a lengthy social process which begins under capitalism. Its starting point is the tendency of capitalism to develop the forces of production (i.e. to raise the productivity of labour and to concentrate the means of production in larger units).

Secondly, capitalism produces its own grave digger, the working class, which grows with the growth of capital.

The first step, the decisive breakthrough to socialism, comes with the conquest of political power by the working class; that is, with the destruction of the capitalist state apparatus and the establishment of a workers' state — what Marx called the dictatorship of the proletariat. By this he meant not a dictatorship *over* the working class but the direction of society by the working class itself. Looking at the Paris Commune of 1871, Marx specified mechanisms through which this could be achieved: the replacement of the parliamentary talk shop by a working body; the election and recallability of all state officials; no official to earn more than a skilled worker's wage; abolition of the standing army and formation of a workers' militia. The Russian revolution showed us the organisational form of workers' power — the *soviet* or workers' council — which arises directly from working-class struggle.

Following the consolidation of its state power and the defeat of the inevitable capitalist attempts at counter-revolution, the working class has to secure the transition to a fully socialist, classless society.

The working class will use its power to take all important industries and businesses into social ownership and place them under workers' control. All the working population will be drawn into administering the new society. This will make democratic planning of the economy possible, ensuring an enormous growth in the wealth of society and that this growth serves people's needs.

It will liberate women by establishing their complete legal equality and by socialising the burden of housework and child care so that this formal equality becomes reality. It will free society from the stains of racial, sexual and national bigotry.

It will use the enormous advances of modern science and technology to eliminate the dangers and drudgery of work. It will systematically reduce the working week and simultaneously raise the educational and cultural level of the people. This will pave the way for the disappearance of any group of privileged experts and for overcoming the divisions between mental and manual labour.

It will steadily widen the range of goods and services available free of charge — a process leading to the disappearance of money and to distribution on the principle, *'each according to their needs'*.

All this must be done in conjunction with spreading the revolution internationally. We know from the Russian experience that the transition to socialism cannot be completed in one country.

Once this has been achieved and capitalism has been destroyed worldwide, the immense resources of our planet will be harnessed for the peoples' needs. The state will wither away for lack of anyone to repress or privilege to protect. A new epoch of human history will open — the epoch of real freedom for a united humanity.

But you can't change human nature . . .

So what is the most common objection to this vision of socialism?

'Socialism will never work, you can't change human nature.'

Before answering this point directly, it's worth noting just *how* this argument is used. Whenever conservatives are confronted with protests against exploitation and oppression, they always turn to the human nature argument. War? Well it's human nature to fight. Racism? It's human nature to fear 'outsiders' and people who are 'different'. The oppression of women? Human nature again: men and women are 'naturally different'.

Slavery, too, was once supposed to be a product of human nature. It was the nature of blacks, it was said, to be slaves. The same with feudalism, and usually God was brought into back up the argument. Remember the words of the hymn:

The rich man in his castle
The poor man at his gate
God made them high and lowly
And ordered their estate.

It was the God-given nature of some people to be lords and others to be serfs. 'Human nature', God-given or otherwise, has always been the favourite alibi of the oppressors.

But what is this unchanging human nature supposed to be? Clearly human beings do have certain more or less fixed and permanent needs. To survive at all they need air, food, drink, shelter, etc. They also have sexual and emotional needs. To live humanly, rather than just exist, they need social contact, affection, love and a measure of freedom. However none of these features of human nature will cause the slightest problems for socialism. On the contrary, socialism will meet these permanent human needs immeasurably better than capitalism or any other previous form of society.

But of course this is not what people mean when they bring up the question of human nature. They mean that human beings are 'naturally' selfish and greedy and this will make a society of solidarity and equality impossible.

Again it is important to know the source of this idea. It comes from the Christian doctrine of original sin and has no scientific basis whatsoever. In fact even in our present society it's not difficult to observe numerous acts of kindness, generosity and self-sacrifice which would be impossible if people were selfish by nature. But under capitalism these features of the human personality are obscured because a society based on production for profit encourages greed, indeed demands it, at every turn.

More generally, the point is that it is the material social conditions in which people live that shape their personality and behaviour. As Marx put it, human nature is nothing but 'the ensemble of social relations'. The proof of this is seen in the enormous differences in what people in different societies have thought of as 'natural'.

To the American Indian, private ownership of land was 'unnatural'. To the 18th-century landowner it was the most basic human right. To the Ancient Greeks, homosexuality was the highest form of love. To the Victorian Englishman it was the lowest. To the traditional Hindu, arranged marriage has been the norm for centuries. To most Westerners it now seems 'unnatural'. Change the social conditions and you change 'human nature'.

Even more important is Marx's point that it is not just that changed circumstances produce changed people, but that people change *in the process* of changing their circumstances. You can see this in an ordinary strike. Most strikes begin because workers want more money. But as the strike goes on, feelings of solidarity and collective pride often grow and become just as important as the original issue.

Revolution is a strike writ large. In a revolution millions of people stand up for the first time and take control of their society. Their 'human nature' will grow accordingly. 'Revolution is necessary', wrote Marx, 'not only because the ruling class cannot be overthrown in any other way, but also because the class overthrowing it can only in a revolution succeed in ridding itself of all the muck of ages and become fitted to found society anew.'

Won't we always need bosses?

'Workers' control? It would never work. Workers are too stupid to run industry. Someone always has to be boss.'

This familiar objection to the very basis of socialism contains a mixture of elements. In large part it is just anti-working class prejudice of the kind that is widespread in the middle class, almost universal in the ruling class, and unfortunately not unknown in the working class itself. But it also points to a real problem, not an insoluble problem, but a problem nevertheless.

First let's deal with the prejudice. The fact is that most workers as individuals, and even more so as a collective, know far more about the immediate process of production than does the management hierarchy above them. After all it is they who actually do the work. The main function of foremen, supervisors, managers, etc. is not to tell workers *how* to do the job, but to ensure that they do it. They are 'necessary' for the simple reason that in a system based on exploitation workers have an entirely reasonable inclination to do as little alienated labour as possible. Many of the other 'special skills' of management — advertising, marketing, winning contracts by wining and dining other executives, devising productivity schemes, 'handling' strikes and disputes and so on — flow from the requirements of production organised on a capitalist basis.

In a socialist society these special skills would become as redundant as medieval jousting is now.

It must also be remembered that much of the knowledge required for running industry that workers lack has nothing whatsoever to do with their lack of ability. It is simply kept secret from them because employers think — rightly — that it wouldn't be 'safe' for trade unionists, shop stewards etc. to know what is going on.

The main obstacle to workers' control, apart from capitalist power, is not workers' lack of knowledge but their lack of confidence in their own abilities. This is hardly surprising for the whole capitalist system, through its schools, its media, its bureaucracies and officials, operates to crush this confidence.

However it is the struggle for workers' control, the revolution itself, which will remove this obstacle. In revolution workers discover their power, and their confidence soars. The day after they have smashed the state, the prospect of running British Leyland won't seem so daunting.

So much for the prejudice. What then is the real problem? Class society creates a division between manual and mental labour and capitalism accentuates this division. Moreover, capitalism fragments production itself into innumerable small repetitive operations performed by different workers. The result is that, in general, workers do not have the scientific and technical knowledge needed for *complete* mastery of the production process, nor will they have it immediately following the revolution. Consequently many of the 'experts' who are highly privileged in relation to ordinary workers will still be needed in the first stages of workers' power. Indeed it may prove necessary to retain their co-operation by continuing to offer them certain limited privileges.

Does this undermine the possibility of workers' control? No, because even if the experts remain, they can still be placed under the control of the workers. Under *capitalism* technical specialists are highly paid, but they don't actually run enterprises. They work for managers and employers who may have little technical knowledge, but who can judge the work of the specialists by how it contributes to their profits. Under *workers' power* the specialists will still work for managers and employers — but the managers will be the elected factory council and the employer will be the workers' state. These bodies may lack technical knowledge, but will judge the work of the specialists by how it contributes to social need.

Workers' control therefore *is* a practical proposition. Indeed, looking at the current state of British and world industry, it is the only practical proposition.

Don't revolutions mean violence?

It is certainly likely that a revolution would involve some violence for the simple reason that the ruling class is not going to surrender its wealth and power peacefully. For the same reason, to reject revolution because it involves violence is to reject the possibility of getting rid of capitalism. And however much violence there would be in a revolution, it pales into insignificance compared with the violence involved in allowing capitalism to continue.

Capitalism is inseparable from violence and generates it at every turn. Thus the daily process of capitalist production exposes workers to injury, disease and even death — all in the pursuit of profit. There is the violence of condemning thousands of millions to poverty, and hundreds of millions to starvation in a world overflowing with wealth. There is the violence of military dictatorship — the only form in which capitalism can survive in many parts of the world, and the violence of imperialism which supports and maintains it.

There is the violence of capitalist war which has claimed at least 100 million victims this century and which threatens the ultimate violence of the nuclear holocaust.

No system based on the exploitation of the overwhelming majority by a tiny minority can maintain itself without violence. No system based on the competitive struggle for profits, one firm against another, one country's firms against another's, can avoid war. The only way to end this ongoing violence is for the working class to use the collective violence of revolution to overthrow capitalism. But having said this, it's still important to challenge the capitalist image of revolution as an orgy of mindless bloodletting.

Revolution is violent. It is the forcible imposition of the will of one section of the population, the working majority, on the other, the ruling minority. But precisely because it *is* a question of the majority repressing the minority rather than the other way around, it is likely to involve relatively little bloodshed.

The bourgeoisie cannot fight its *own* battles; it is numerically weak. It depends on others, basically workers in uniform, to fight for it. All the violence the ruling class inflicts on the working class is done by one section of the workers against the rest. A powerful working-class movement that is united, ready to fight, and correctly led, can prevent this. It can break the power of the ruling class by winning over the rank and file of the army. When this happens the ruling class is unable to mount the level of resistance which would necessitate the use of very extensive violence by workers. It was because just such a process had taken place in the Russian revolution of 1917 that the October insurrection in Petrograd cost only a handful of lives.

It is also important to remember that revolutions don't begin with acts of violence by revolutionaries. They arise from the class struggle itself and erupt when the class antagonisms in capitalism boil over.

If, however, the working class fails to use the necessary force at the decisive moment, then it lays itself open to the immeasurably greater violence of capitalist repression. Thus, during the Paris Commune of 1871, 30,000 Communards were slaughtered in a few days. The fascist counter-revolutions of Italy, Germany and Spain took the lives of millions. The Chilean coup of ten years ago and the Polish coup of 1981 show the same basic feature. In all these cases the failure to press home the revolution is punished by a one-sided civil war of hideous violence and barbarity.

Anyone put off revolution because of its alleged 'violence' is simply being duped by the utterly hypocritical arguments of bourgeois politicians who preach 'non-violence' to the workers, but never practice it themselves.

'Under socialism they'd make us all the same . . .'

'Under socialism everyone will be the same.' 'Socialism means grey uniformity.' 'Socialism denies freedom of choice to the individual.'

This is a litany of complaint that must be familiar to every socialist. But before answering it, let's consider the record of capitalism on this question, for supporters of capitalism have always claimed the defence of individuality and individual freedom as its supreme virtues.

In fact individuality under capitalism has always been the preserve of the privileged few. From school uniform and rote-learning to army uniform and square-bashing, from terraced housing and tower blocks to production lines and typing pools, the tendency of capitalism is precisely to impose 'grey uniformity' on the working class. It is the same in the fields of art, entertainment and sport. Capitalism produces the 'spectator' and the 'mass audience' — the majority of the population reduced to the role of passive observers to the activities of a few 'stars' purveyed by a centralised mass media.

All this derives from the fundamental features of the system — its divisions into classes and its organisation of production for profit. The fact that the ruling class is a tiny minority of society means that it can survive only by maintaining the working class majority in a state of mass conformity. The organisation of production for profit means that the individual creative labour of millions is stripped of its individuality and creativity and turned into so many hours of abstract labour power. Competition compels the capitalist to treat workers not as human beings but as items in the accounts, as mere appendages to machines. The individualism of capitalism was always only the individualism of the enterpreneurs — their freedom to exploit and accumulate without regard to social need.

But even this individualism is largely a thing of the past. In the age of the giant bureaucratic corporation the capitalist manager also becomes just a conforming cog in the accumulation machine.

The bogey of Stalinist Russia is always raised here as an example of 'socialism' crushing all individual freedom. But Russia is not socialist but state capitalist — a highly centralised form of exploitation which is an extreme expression of the anti-individualist tendency inherent in capitalism.

Marxists, it must be emphasised, are *not* opposed to individualism as such, only to bourgeois individualism which operates at the expense of the rest of society. Individualism that *contributes* to society, that makes it more varied, lively and humane, is something we are all in favour of.

The starting point of socialism is the *collective* action of workers. But that collective action is simultaneously an increase in the *individual* activity and freedom of each worker involved. It is the means through which the individual workers can assert their needs, stand up for their rights, refuse to be just entries on a balance sheet and begin to control their own lives.

The victory of the socialist revolution would raise this individual freedom twofold. Through workers' councils each individual would participate in running society. Through workers' control each individual would shape his or her working environment. Through the provision of proper contraception, abortion and nursery facilities women would be able to make a free individual choice about having children. With equal pay and work for all, marriage and sexual relationships would also become a matter of free choice rather than economic dependence.

Through the abolition of poverty and the drastic reduction of the working week, each individual would be free to develop his or her talents to the full. Indeed, one of the main reasons for fighting for socialism is precisely to secure a society in which, as Marx put it in **The Communist Manifesto**, 'the free development of each is the condition of the free development of all'.

Chapter Two:
So how do we get to this new world?

LOOK AT human history and you will see a tale of misery. Exploitation and oppression, barbarous cruelty, rebellion and repression, the horror of war — for thousands of years these have not been the exception but the rule.

On the one hand a tiny minority have lived in all the luxury and splendour the times would allow. On the other a perpetual majority — the poor — have waged a life-long struggle simply to survive.

This is one side of history but not the only side. It can also be seen as the triumphant march of human progress, the ceaseless expansion of humanity's productive capacities, of knowledge and of the ability to harness the natural environment to make life better, freer, more human.

The point is that up to now these two sides of history have seemed inseparable. The amazing growth of the productive forces, the staggering advances in science and technology have not lessened the barbarities inflicted by humans on humans, but refined and perfected them. The enormous increase in the collective material wealth of the world has not narrowed the gap between rich and poor. To look at the world today — the world of modern capitalism — is to see these age-old contradictions pushed to their extreme limits. On one side live the millionaires and billionaires jet-setting from one luxury watering hole to another, on the other are the hideous shanty towns of Calcutta, Sao Paolo or Manila, and the emaciated famine victims of Ethiopia.

And then, of course, there is the final madness: great scientific breakthroughs which reveal the structure of the atom and are put to a hideous application — nuclear weapons.

What distinguishes Marxism from all other theories and ideologies, past and present, is that it has identified a *realistic* way out of this impasse. A way of abolishing class divisions, of ending exploitation and war, of freeing the world's workers from unending poverty and drudgery — a way forward for the human race. The key word here is *realistic*, for the aspiration to freedom and equality long predates Marxm.

From Spartacus onwards the oppressed have rebelled against their oppression, and thinkers have dreamed of a harmonious society. Christianity itself, like all religions, is a distorted expression of these aspirations.

What Marx did, and was the first to do, was to place these aspirations on a scientific foundation. He showed that human emancipation was actually possible, not on the basis of his or anyone else's special plan or divine inspiration, but on the basis of forces and tendencies already at work in society.

Above all, Marx showed that capitalism itself produced a social force — the working class — whose conditions not only drove it to rebel but gave it the capacity to overthrow capitalism and put an end to all forms of class rule.

This — the workers' struggle for freedom — is the heart of Marxism, its essential message for all those who want to change the world. Lenin put it this way: 'The main thing in the teaching of Marx is the elucidation of the world-wide historical role of the proletariat as the builder of a socialist society.'

Why we don't like Mondays

'Roll on Friday'. This familiar phrase expresses the fact that for most of us the work we do is tedious and meaningless. We wish away our lives clock-watching because we only begin to feel free when we are not at work.

The content of our work, what we actually make or do, is of secondary importance. We do it neither to meet our own needs, nor the needs of others, but simply to earn a living, not as part of our real life activity, but an unavoidable means to carry on with life. Marx recognised that work under capitalism is like this. He called it 'alienated labour', and he showed it was bound up with wage labour. Wage labour ensures that most people have to sell their ability to work to those who control the means of production.

Labour — alienated or not — is the very foundation of society. What is produced and how that production is organised are the basic factors shaping the course of history. The simple fact, as Engels put it, 'is that mankind must first of all eat, drink, have shelter and clothing before it can pursue science, art, religion, etc.' This is such a simple statement that it is worth considering for a moment why it remained hidden for so long.

First, because for thousands of years the people who actually worked were always the lowest stratum of society. The significance of their work could be ignored. Secondly, because those who run society, slave-owners, landlords, industrialists or bankers, do no productive work themselves, they can flatter themselves that it's their decrees and commands which make society tick. Moreover, they have an interest in ensuring the rest of us believe this too. Hence the 'great man' view of history taught in schools. In contrast it was precisely because Marx had grasped the potential of the working class to master society that he was able to see the real importance of labour.

Marx distinguished two aspects of work. Firstly, he focussed on the actual business of making things, the use of tools to transform raw material into products that can be consumed to sustain human life. A society's capacity to do this he called its *forces of production*. Secondly, Marx analysed relationships between people that are necessary for production to take place. These relationships involve both co-operation, as when a tribe goes out to hunt, and subordination, as between worker and capitalist. They are called by Marx the *relations of production*.

The level reached by the forces of production conditions the relations of production. The earliest stage of the productive forces, the use of primitive tools for hunting, gave rise to the tribe. The development of the extensive cultivation of land produced the social relations of slavery and then serfdom. The growth of trade, manufacture and then industry produced the dominant production relation of wage labour. The sum total of these relations of production within society Marx called the 'mode of production'.

Marx pointed to four such modes of production (he called them the Asiatic, ancient, feudal and capitalist) as the main periods in past history. The fifth, socialism, he predicted as the coming epoch.

What do you mean by exploitation?

What happens when workers sell their labour power to the capitalist? The employer gets the worker's labour for a certain number of hours, and in return the worker receives a wage. It seems a fair deal — a certain amount of money is exchanged for a certain amount of labour. Both sides agree to the arrangement; exchange is no robbery.

'Exploitation' is said to be something that occurs only exceptionally, when the employer somehow cheats the workers. The popularity of the slogan 'A fair day's wage for a fair day's work' shows that many workers also accept this view.

Marx, however, showed that exploitation was not the exception but the rule, and that it was built into wage labour. He began by analysing the 'commodity', for under capitalism both capital and labour power are 'commodities', goods produced for exchange.

Commodities come in all shapes and sizes, and serve a large variety of purposes. They can be anything from an ocean liner to a packet of cornflakes. Yet they can all (through money) be exchanged for each other. This is only possible because they have one thing in common — they are all the products of definite amounts of human labour time. The value of a commodity is determined by the amount of labour time society has to spend on producing it. (Marx calls this 'socially necessary labour time'.)

Now apply this 'labour theory of value' to the commodity of labour power itself. The value of labour power is also determined by the amount of labour time needed to produce it — that is, by what it takes to feed, clothe, house, educate and reproduce the worker. The worker's wages pay for the cost of 'producing' the worker's ability to work. In this sense the buying of labour power is a 'fair' exchange like any other.

But labour power is different from all other commodities. It is *creative*. It produces *more* value than it takes to maintain itself. (If human labour didn't produce more than it consumed there would have been no development of the productive forces and no history.) But this 'surplus' value goes to the capitalist, not the worker.

Thus if a worker sells, say, 40 hours of labour time to the capitalist and is paid £100, enough to support him or her for that week, he or she will produce £100 worth of goods in, say, only 20 hours. The remaining 20 hours of the working week will be unpaid labour for the capitalist.

The unpaid labour is the hidden secret of capitalist exploitation. Beneath the apparent 'fair' exchange, it is the source of all profit. For in those extra 20 hours — the figure will of course vary with the circumstances — the worker will produce *another* £100 worth of goods for the capitalist. This Marx called 'surplus value'. It is the capitalist's profit.

Marx's theory of surplus value does more than prove that capitalism is based on exploitation. It also reveals the irreconcilable conflict of interest that lies at the heart of the system and divides it into warring classes. Driven by competition, capitalists seek always to extend the unpaid labour time they extract from the workers. Driven by human need, the workers seek to reduce it. Hence — on one side — speed-ups, productivity deals, wages cuts; and on the other side wage demands, strikes and the whole trade union struggle.

The only solution to the conflict is for the workers to go beyond struggle over the *role* of exploitation, and abolish it by seizing the means of production and ending the sale of labour power.

What is 'capital'?

Capitalism is a system dominated by capital. But what is capital? The everyday view, which quite suits our rulers, is that capital is simply a large amount of money, machinery and other means of production. From this it appears that you can't have any production without capital, and capitalism seems to be an eternal system.

Marx, however, penetrated beneath this appearance to show that capital is not just a thing (money, machines, etc.) but also a social relationship, a relation of production. Capital doesn't grow on trees, it has to be produced. Capital is therefore 'stored up' or 'accumulated labour'. (Marx also calls it dead labour.) But stored-up labour is necessary for any system of production, including socialism — it only becomes *capital* in certain social relations.

Firstly, stored-up labour becomes capital when it can be exchanged with the live labour power of workers in a way which increases the value of that stored-up labour. For capitalism to develop there must be a class of people who have been separated from the means of production, and are therefore forced to sell their ability to work to those who own and control the means of production.

Capital, therefore, implies wage labour. They are two sides of the same equation.

Secondly, capital can only exist as many capitals, in other words as production units working separately and in competition with each other. It is this competition which compels those who possess stored-up labour to use it as capital, to strive to expand its value by employing workers, rather than just consuming it themselves. Henry Ford isn't driven to make more and more profits by personal greed alone, but by competition with General Motors, Fiat, Volkswagen and other giant car firms.

Production for production's sake, accumulation for accumulation's sake. This is the basic dynamic of capitalism.

The question of private ownership is of secondary importance. It was the typical form in which capitalism developed, but as long as the workers are separated from the means of production, and as long as the minority who control those means of production are compelled by competition to increase their value and exploit their workers, you still have capital and capitalism.

State-owned British Steel and BL are just as much capitalist enterprises as privately-owned Unilever or ICI. State-owned USSR Ltd is just as capitalist as partially state-owned Great Britain Ltd.

Capitalism is therefore a system in which the living labour of workers is only a means to increase accumulated labour. Living labour is dominated by dead labour. The worker is an appendage to the machine. Socialism, through social ownership and workers' control, will reverse this relationship. Accumulated labour will serve living labour. Production will be for need not profit.

How capitalism causes crises

Capitalism is a system of recurring economic crises. At the moment we're living through the latest of these. To the ruling class and its hangers-on — its journalists, politicians, economists and the rest — the explanations for these crises vary. Sometimes they are seen as accidents, sometimes as 'acts of God' like the weather, sometimes greedy workers are to blame, and sometimes government mismanagement.

What is always clear is that the working class suffers most. Unemployment officially passed the two million mark in 1980. We have now had years of mass unemployment, on a scale comparable to the 1930s, and there is no end in sight. With the real number of unemployed well over four million there can hardly be a working-class family whose lives are not directly or indirectly affected by the misery of the dole queue.

The Marxist explanation of unemployment starts from the fact that capitalist production is production for profit. It follows from this that under capitalism people are only employed when their employment, directly or indirectly, assists in the making of profits. When it ceases to do so they cease to be employed.

The key to the overall level of employment at any time is therefore the average rate of profit across industry as a whole. When the average rate of profit is high capitalists are keen to invest, to expand their operations, to launch new projects and to take on new labour. When the average rate of profit is low, capitalists are reluctant to invest; old industries becomes out of date and uncompetitive for lack of new plant and are forced to close; new industries fail to take their place. Unemployment rises.

Each of these situations creates a certain momentum of its own. When new workers are taken on they have more money to spend. Demand for goods increases and production rises to meet the demand. Yet more workers are then employed to raise production, and so on. On the other hand, when unemployment rises workers on the dole have less to spend. Demand for goods falls, production falls and more workers are made redundant. There is a slump.

The key question is what makes the rate of profit high or low in the first place? What decides whether the economy spirals upwards into boom or downwards into slump? There are two processes at work here. The first is cyclical. It causes the system to alternate, more or less regularly, from boom to slump and back again. In the boom the increased demand for labour enables workers to push up wages to the point where they cut into profits. The rate of profit falls and the boom collapses into slump. In the slump unemployment cuts the bargaining power of workers and wages fall until eventually the rate of profit is restored. The slump turns into boom.

The second process is more fundamental. It is an underlying long-run tendency for the rate of profit to fall.

Because capitalism is competitive, each capitalist unit strives to produce as much as possible, to grab as large a share of the market as it can. But because it is exploitative, it never pays the workers enough for them to buy up all the goods they produce. As a result, it is always faced with the danger of overproduction — of producing more than can be sold.

Capitalism cannot solve this problem by raising wages, because that would cut into its profits. What *is* a solution to this problem is for capitalists themselves continually to reinvest their profits by producing ever more 'means of production': more machines, and machines for making more machines. This can work as long as the capitalists invest, and this they will do only as long as it produces profits.

However, this investment in means of production itself contributes to a long-term tendency for the rate of profit to fall. The reason is that profit itself derives only from the exploitation of labour power — from the living labour of workers, not from the accumulated labour represented by machines. As capitalists buy more and more machinery, the amount of living labour becomes a proportionally smaller part of the capitalist's outlay (we have seen this happen enormously in our own time as computers have enabled one worker to perform the task previously done by several).

The result is that the rate of profit — the amount of profit in relation to the capitalist's total outlay — declines, even though the capitalist will try to counter-balance this by driving the workers harder or for longer hours.

Once the rate of profit falls below a certain level, capitalists lose the incentive to invest and the system faces a crisis of overproduction as 'means of production' go unbought — machinery goes unsold, factory buildings and office blocks stand empty. This spirals into recession and slump, firms go bankrupt, workers are laid off, and unemployment soars.

There are a number of factors which can offset the falling rate of profit. In the heyday of British imperialism, for example, huge amounts of capital were exported to pre-capitalist countries — which meant there was less capital to invest in Britain, so less danger of overproduction. The destruction of even larger amounts of capital in war, or by permanent high levels of spending on armaments during peacetime, can also stave off, for a period, the growth of capital in proportion to labour power.

Economic crisis itself destroys or devalues a lot of capital by bankrupting the weaker firms. That makes possible a higher rate of profit for those who survive. This is why capitalism generally alternates between boom and slump and why the system was capable of sustained growth in the 1880s and '90s and, even more so, in the period 1950-73.

Sooner or later, however, this very growth ensures that the basic tendency for the rate of profit to fall reasserts itself. It's just such a fall which underlies the present world recession. Moreover, the fact that today's units of capital are both larger and more concentrated than in the past makes it much more difficult for them to simply go bankrupt. When Britain had a dozen or more car manufacturers, one or two could be sacrificed in a recession to the advantage of the rest. Today BL, the only remaining car firm, cannot be allowed to go under without the risk of irreparable damage to the rest of the economy.

The result is that capitalism finds it more difficult to use a short, sharp crisis to destroy sections of capital and so restore the rate of profit. Instead we have a somewhat less sharp collapse. But one which drags on and on without hope of any recovery.

The tendency of the rate of profit to decline is a fundamental and insoluble contradiction of capitalism. It is a concrete expression of the fact that capitalist relations of production have become a barrier to humanity's further development of its productive forces. Mass unemployment is a result of contradictions built into the very nature of capitalism, of a system based on the search for profit. Only when production is for need, not profit, will humanity be free of economic crises and the untold misery they cause, free to move forward.

Where is history leading?

The basis of society is production. Social relations between people, the form of law and government, depend ultimately on the ability of humanity to produce the necessities of life. *This is the first premise of Marx's theory of history. But how can one mode of production be transformed into another?*

It cannot be done simply by will. Nor is it just a matter of convincing people that it's a good idea. For Marx the first basis for such a change is that, within a particular mode of production, the forces of production should have developed to a level where new relationships of production become possible. Until this has happened all revolutions are doomed to fail.

But once the productive forces have reached this level, the existing relations of production become reactionary. They hold back the further development of society and are ready to be overturned.

Capitalism has long since reached this stage. It has created a world economy and a world division of labour. It has raised productivity to the point that the working day could be drastically reduced. It has increased production to the point where, potentially, there is more than enough to ensure a decent life for all.

But the continued existence of capitalist relations of production prevents this potential being realised. The division of society into bosses and workers, and the competitive struggle between bosses for profits, ensures that poverty and starvation continue, that working hours remain long, and that the world remains divided into hostile, warring states.

The fact that capitalism is still with us shows that the development of the productive forces doesn't, by itself, change the system. Relations of production are *class* relations. They imply a ruling class which controls production — and an oppressed class (or classes) that produces. The ruling class has a vested interest in maintaining the reactionary relations of production. Changing the mode of production involves a struggle by the oppressed class that is linked to, and embodies, the rising forces of production, to overthrow the ruling class. The motor of history, therefore, is class struggle.

The change from feudalism to capitalism was one example of this process. It involved a struggle by the middle class — or bourgeoisie — supported by other oppressed classes, to destroy the power of the monarchy and sweep away the feudal restrictions which were blocking the development of capitalism. The decisive moments in that struggle were two great revolutions: the English Revolution of 1642 and the French Revolution of 1789.

The change from capitalism to socialism will be another example. It will involve the struggle of the working class, at the head of all the oppressed, to destroy the power of the bourgeoisie and establish social control of production. Its decisive moment will also be a revolution.

The advance to socialism, however, is far from inevitable. Human history is no mere mechanical process — its advance, or retreat, depends upon the collective class actions and decisions of human beings. Friedrich Engels once wrote: 'Capitalist society faces a dilemma, either an advance to socialism or a reversion to barbarism.' What happens depends on the outcome of class struggle.

Socialism or barbarism?

One possible product of capitalism in crisis has already revealed itself once this century: fascism, with the Nazi domination of much of Europe, brought war, devastation, and the extermination of millions of people simply because they belonged to a different race, nationality, or political persuasion.

At the moment the fascists are isolated, fragmented and confined to the margins of the political scene. But this doesn't mean that we can sink into a complacent 'it can't happen here' attitude. Only a few years ago, before it was thrown back by the Anti-Nazi League, the British National Front was a growing threat. In Germany, in 1928, Hitler's Nazis seemed insignificant. Yet within five years they were in power, and one has only to look at Mitterrand's France to see a neo-Nazi movement making rapid advances.

For all these reasons an analysis of fascism remains an essential weapon in the Marxist theoretical arsenal. It is also essential that this analysis should be precise. It mustn't blur the distinction between real fascism and every other form of right-wing authoritarianism. Such confusion not only spreads unnecessary panic but also leads to an *underestimation* of the brutality and danger of the real thing.

The first point to be made in analysing fascism is that it is not some collective madness that suddenly seizes the whole of society. Nor is it a freak of the German (or Italian) national character, or the product of the evil genius of a demonic charismatic leader. Nor on the other hand is it just *any* violation of democracy or human rights (under capitalism such violations occur all the time). Rather, fascism is a phenomenon generated by the very nature of capitalism, but which has quite specific class roots. In power, it is a form of bourgeois rule sharply different from ordinary capitalist democracy in that it involves the annihilation of all independent working-class organisations.

The class basis of fascism is, in the first place, the petty bourgeoisie — small shopkeepers, self-employed and the like — and it is from here that the core of a fascist movement is recruited. The petty bourgeoisie feels crushed between big capital on the one hand and the organised working class on the other. In times of severe economic crisis this double pressure becomes more acute and, under the threat of mass bankruptcy, the petty bourgeoisie searches desperately for a way out.

If in this situation the working class, under revolutionary leadership, shows its capacity and determination to resolve the crisis it can draw large sections of the middle class behind it. If, however, the working class fails to give a clear lead then the petty bourgeoisie can swing wildly to the right and turn to fascism.

This is because the ideology of fascism appears to reflect the experience of the enraged petty bourgeoisie. It combines vague rhetoric against international finance with bitter hostility to the labour movement. These contradictory attitudes are cemented together by the racist fantasy that international capitalism and communism are parts of a world conspiracy to undermine the purity of race and nation. (In Germany the Nazis made the Jews their victims; the British National Front in the 1970s tried to blame black people.)

The petty bourgeoisie, however, cannot become the ruling class in modern capitalism. Consequently fascism — basing itself on this class — cannot come to power solely by its own efforts. It needs the backing of the ruling class itself.

But for the ruling class, fascism is a risky option which involves handing the reins of power to people it regards as vulgar fanatics. It will take this step only in very pressing circumstances. Firstly, the economic crisis must be so severe that the profitability of capitalism cannot be restored without the wholesale destruction of the labour movement. Secondly, the ruling class must have been put in fear of its life by that labour movement. Thirdly, it must be confident that the working class is weak enough for the fascist solution to succeed. It has no desire to provoke its own overthrow.

These conditions are most likely to occur in the aftermath of revolutionary situations that have been wasted by reformist leadership. So it was in Italy in 1921, in Germany in 1933 and in Spain in 1936. The price of failing to make the socialist revolution is horrifically high.

So what puts socialist revolution on the agenda?

What effect does the state of the economy have on the state of the class struggle? Is it necessary for the slump to become even more severe and for workers to be reduced to extreme poverty before there will be mass rebellion against capitalism? Or does there have to be a new boom in order to restore workers' confidence?

These are obviously important questions for Marxism, especially at a time when the working-class movement has been seriously damaged and undermined by mass unemployment. They are also difficult to answer — for there is no simple, mechanical or automatic relationship between economic conditions and the level of working-class resistance. Factors such as the historical traditions of the class, the degree of consciousness and organisation, and the quality of its leadership, all have their effect.

Nevertheless on the basis of previous experience of booms and slumps it is possible to make certain broad generalisations.

First of all, conditions of prolonged boom (such as from the Second World War to the mid-1960s) create favourable conditions for the development of a high level of confidence and organisation. However the readiness and capacity of employers to make concessions restricts the scale of the struggle. Strikes tend to be successful but small and short. There are no class-wide life and death battles. Consequently workers feel no compulsion to generalise the struggle politically, and show little interest in revolutionary socialist ideas. In a period of sustained expansion reforms can be won but capitalism cannot be overthrown.

In contrast, conditions of slump or economic crisis sharply raise the stakes of the struggle. The employers, with the threat of bankruptcy at their backs, are much more determined and more likely to enlist the aid of the state.

To make gains, or even to hold on to the gains of the past, workers have to fight much harder and on a much wider scale. The whole struggle becomes more bitter and more generalised and the question of political leadership becomes much more important. The slump creates the potential for both greater victories (up to and including the overthrow of the system) and greater defeats. Moreover defeats in conditions of mass unemployment are likely to be more demoralising.

In general, revolutionary struggle and revolutionary consciousness combine two elements: bitterness at the exploiters and their system and confidence in the possibility of fighting. The former tends to be a product of the slump, the latter of the boom. We can therefore say that it is neither the boom by itself, nor the slump by itself, that raises the class struggle to its highest level, but rather the rapid alternation between one and the other.

Three variations are possible here. First, a boom in which workers' expectations, confidence and organisation rise, followed by the onset of a slump to which workers respond with mass struggles. Second, a slump in which bitterness accumulates, followed by a boom which gives workers the confidence to fight. And a third possibility is a prolonged crisis with the ruling class continually on the attack and the working class falling back until the former finally overreaches itself and provokes a desperate mass resistance. If this resistance proves successful it can give workers the confidence to return to the offensive.

Situations are possible which combine elements of these three different variations. A small recovery within an overall crisis, for instance, will give some workers slightly more confidence, against a ruling class driven by the crisis to press on and on with its attacks on living standards and thus compelled time and again to risk overreaching itself.

Apart from the 1984-5 miners' strike, the present bosses' offensive in Britain has not met with a serious fightback, and the workers' movement as a whole remains weakened. But the long-term prospects for the ruling class are bleak. Capitalism is not going to return to sustained boom. However, within the continuing crisis there will be repeated oscillations up and down. Each such oscillation carries with it the possibility of an upsurge in the class struggle, as does each new ruling-class assault.

Sooner or later, therefore, the tide will turn, and when it does the stakes will be very high indeed.

What we mean by workers' power

Any well-organised strike needs a strike committee made up of shop stewards or other representatives elected by the rank and file. Its job is to organise picketing, blacking and support from other workers. If the strike spreads throughout the industry or to other industries the strike committee will need to expand to include representatives from all the workers involved, and its tasks and responsibilities will grow too.

If there is a general strike or a succession of mass strikes and occupations, and the working class mounts a serious challenge to the system, then hundreds of such organisations will be needed. And they will face a host of new tasks: calling demonstrations, maintaining essential supplies and transport, defending picket lines and workers' organisations against attack, creating an alternative news service to counteract government propaganda, perhaps the co-ordination of rent strikes and the protection of working-class areas.

Such workers' councils — or '*soviets*', to use the Russian word — have always risen from the needs of the struggle itself — andnot as an abstract scheme imposed by theorists. This was true of the Russian soviets of 1905 and 1917, the workers' councils of the German Revolution 1918-19, those of Spain 1936 and of Hungary 1956.

In the British General Strike there were Councils of Action which could have developed in this direction if the struggle had continued. The inter-factory committees in Poland in 1980, which linked the Gdansk shipyard occupation with hundreds of other workplaces across the country, had the same potential.

Soviets, in taking on many of the functions of government, become alternative centres of power, rivalling those of the state.

This is called 'dual power'. Dual power cannot last long. It will be ended either by ruling-class repression, as in Germany 1919, or Poland 1981, or by workers' revolution as in Russia in 1917.

That revolution will mean destroying the bourgeois state and replacing it with the workers' councils as the basis of the new state power — workers' power, what Marx called 'the dictatorship of the proletariat'. Based on elections in workplaces where collective debate and discussion are possible, the workers' councils will directly represent the interests of the workers as a class. Delegates will be instantly recallable simply by holding mass meeting, in the workplace, and like all state officials they will receive only the average worker's wage.

The councils, in conjunction with factory committees and the trade unions, will place all production under workers' control. They will requisition the hotels, mansions and extra houses of the rich to house the homeless. They will place the millionaire press and TV stations at the disposal of workers' organisations according to their support among the people.

They will organise community nurseries, creches, restaurants and laundries to free women from the oppressive burden of housework. They will put colleges and schools under the control of those who use them, especially the students. The huge waste of resources on fat salaries, pomp and ceremony, Rolls-Royces, banquets and other junketings that accompany the capitalist state, will be ended at a stroke.

Every working person will be able to take part in running the state. By arming the workers and forming workers' militias the new state will be able to mobilise the necessary force to deal with attempts at counter-revolution. But as this threat recedes, as it will in so far as the revolution is able to defeat the capitalists at home and abroad, so these repressive functions of the state will fade, leaving only the organisation of the whole people in pursuit of its needs. The state as such will wither away.

This is the real meaning of workers' power. Contrary to all the propaganda about left totalitarianism, it would be a million times more democratic than any bourgeois parliament, enabling ordinary people, for the first time in history, to take control of their lives.

**Chapter Three:
Getting our ideas right**

But socialists are such a tiny minority . . .

THE MOST obvious obstacle to the socialist transformation of society is the simple fact that most workers are not socialists. Indeed most workers accept capitalism, believe it can't be changed, and view socialists who want to change it as idealists or troublemakers.

So what does Marxism have to say about this crucial problem? Why do workers so often accept reactionary ideas, and how can this change?

It is one of the most basic propositions of Marxism that it is not ideas that shape the state of society, but the state of society that shapes ideas. The generally-held ideas of society reflect the way society is organised. In feudal society there was a rigid division between lords and serfs. This was therefore generally accepted as natural and inevitable; to use the language of the time, something 'ordained by God'. Capitalist society is founded on the profit motive — and therefore *this* is thought of as 'natural'. In fact such ideas do more than simply reflect society; they *justify* it. They justify the current class divisions. As Marxists put it: 'the ruling ideas of any age will be the ideas of the ruling class'.

If we look at capitalism today we can easily see how this can be so. The ruling class controls the channels for the formation and propagation of ideas: the education system, the newspapers, the television stations and all other means of mass communication, and its ideas are dominant in all these. But the power of ruling-class ideas does not arise simply from a 'conspiracy' of rich newspaper proprietors, publishers and university professors, ministers and civil servants and so on. Capitalist ideas seem to make sense because they reflect the world as we experience it. Businesses *are* run for profit and society *is* divided into classes — so to believe these things are 'natural' and 'true' seems simple common sense.

So for Marxists there is nothing particularly surprising about the working-class Tory or the sexist trade unionist. If capitalist ideology didn't dominate workers' thinking in this way capitalism couldn't survive at all.

Similarly socialist ideas will only acquire such 'obviousness' when a socialist society exists. So this faces us with an immediate dilemma: if, as we say, socialism cannot be created *on behalf of* workers, but must be the act of the working class itself, how can this happen when the working class is dominated by capitalist ideas?

Workers' ideas clearly cannot simply be changed on a mass scale by socialist propaganda. A socialist newspaper such as **Socialist Worker** can't match the operations of the millionaire press. The spread of socialist ideas on a mass scale must have a material base; just as capitalist ideas dominate workers' thinking because they reflect their daily experience, so the spread of socialist ideas will reflect changes in that daily experience.

Here it is necessary to clear up a widespread confusion. It is often supposed that the more people suffer, the more revolutionary they become. But if this were so, then the revolution would have happened long ago. In fact it is not suffering, but the experience of *fighting against* suffering that forms the material basis for the growth of socialist ideas.

If the level of workers' struggle is low, and results largely in defeat, then workers — with little control over their own working lives — feel that society cannot be changed. But if the level of struggle is high, and victory follows victory, then workers' confidence in their ability to change their own lives rises, and they become more able to see that alternatives to capitalism are possible. If the level of class struggle is so high that it threatens the existence of the bourgeois state, then socialist ideas can spread like wildfire.

None of this means that the attempt by socialists to spread their ideas through newspapers, pamphlets and books is irrelevant or unnecessary. Workers do not have to be socialists *before* they engage in battles that challenge the ruling class — but their ability to *win* those battles is closely linked to their level of politicial consciousness. Mass strikes, workplace occupations and demonstrations create conditions in which it is possible for socialist ideas to spread, but — as the example of the trade union Solidarity in Poland proves — it is impossible for workers to improvise, suddenly and in the heat of battle, a fully worked-out socialist understanding of the world.

The socialist ideas have to be there, ready to inform those struggles, to articulate and generalise from these new experiences, and ready to prove their practical relevance by pointing to the way forward.

Dialectical materialism? What on earth does that mean?

Marxism is a general theory of society from the point of view of the working class. It includes and integrates into a single whole theories of history, economics, politics and philosophy.

The philosophy of Marxism is usually called 'dialectical materialism'. Marxism is materialist since it regards the production of the necessities of life as the basis on which ideas arise, rather than vice versa. But what does dialectical mean?

There is a difficulty here because it is obviously not a term used in everyday speech, nor, naturally, is it explained in school. It is a philosophical term deriving originally from ancient Greece, and developed by the great German philosopher Hegel at the end of the 18th century.

Dialectics is the logic of change, of evolution and of development. Its starting point is the idea (and the fact) that everything changes and is involved in an ongoing process of coming into being and ceasing to be.

To understand the significance of this compare it with what is known as 'formal' logic (originally developed by Aristotle and usually thought of as the rules of sound thinking). The basic idea of formal logic is that something either is the case or is not the case, but that it can't be both at the same time. For example, the cat is either on the mat or is not on the mat.

For many purposes formal logic is useful and necessary. But as soon as you take movement and change into account, it ceases to be adequate. A cat moving goes through a moment when it is in the process of passing onto the mat or in the process of passing off it — when it is both on and off the mat. Dialectics is in advance of formal logic because it enables us to grasp this contradiction.

This really matters when we come to analyse social development and, in particular, how the transition takes place from one form of society to another. Ruling classes believe in the fixed eternal nature of their form of society. The feudal lords believed feudalism was ordained by God and would last forever. Today's ruling classes believe capitalism reflects a fixed human nature and will similarly survive forever. Dialectics, however, insists that nothing is fixed or lasts forever. Feudalism arose historically and was destroyed historically. Likewise capitalism is a historical product with a beginning and, sooner or later, an end.

This brings us to the second fundamental proposition of dialectics. This is that social change occurs through internal contradiction, through the struggle of opposites. A given society forms a whole or totality, but within that whole there are antagonisms and opposing forces. The change from one form of society to another is the result of the dominant element being overcome by its antagonist or opposite.

It is no accident that dialectics was developed by Hegel at the time of the French Revolution — the greatest, most radical social upheaval the world had then seen. The dialectical theory of development through contradiction was the philosophical expression of the French Revolution.

But because the French Revolution was a bourgeois revolution, one led by lawyers and intellectuals, it necessarily appeared to Hegel that the driving force of history was the struggle between opposite *ideas* (between the idea of monarchy and the idea of a republic, between the idea of aristocracy and the idea of equality, etc.). Marx, coming 50 years later and taking the standpoint of the working class, was able to go beyond Hegel and show that this struggle of ideas was a reflection of a struggle of material forces. With Marx the dialectic became the logic of class struggle.

A third proposition of dialectics is that quantitative changes become qualitative ones. Within a particular framework of society changes occur. With capitalism, for example, the forces of production advance and grow bigger and the working class grows more powerful. For a time these changes are quantitative — they modify society but don't transform it. But sooner or later the changes become too great to be confined within the existing framework. For development to continue, this framework has to be broken and a new social order established.

Thus dialectics is not only the logic of change and of class struggle, but also the logic of revolution. Despite its obscure philosophical origins, it is a powerful practical tool enabling Marxists to grasp the inner dynamics of the working-class struggle.

Their truth, and ours

'We hold these truths to be self evident, that all men are created equal, that they are endowed by their Creator with certain inalienable Rights, that among these are Life, Liberty, and the pursuit of Happiness.'

These celebrated lines from the American Declaration of Independence are typical of the ringing proclamations produced by the bourgeois revolutions that paved the way for the development of modern capitalism — typical in three ways.

First, they concentrate on supposedly universal and absolute, but abstract, truths and rights, rather than on anything specific. Second, in the context of the times, when absolute monarchy was the order of the day in most of the world, they were immensely progressive and genuinely radical. Third, even at the time of writing they were being systematically violated by their bourgeois revolutionary authors — the independent United States continued to practice and tolerate slavery for another ninety years.

Today capitalist propaganda and ideology continue, rather perfunctorily, to proclaim these same universal principles, but the practical violations remain, and the radical progressive content has long since disappeared.

Marx, as the theorist of working-class revolution, developed an entirely different attitude to both 'truth' and 'rights'. For Marx there are no absolute or universal truths, for in the last analysis the test of truth is always practice. A proposition is true in so far as it enables human beings to perform certain practical operations in the world. 'Truth' is therefore historical and above all concrete. A proposition is true in relation to specific circumstances. Change the circumstances sufficiently and it ceases to be true.

Similarly with 'rights'. For Marxists there are no god-given rights that all human beings are born with. People, or more particularly groups and classes, have only such rights as they are able to win and defend in struggle.

Whether or not Marxists support these 'rights' depends on which classes are involved and what they will use the 'rights' to do. Thus we are for 'the right to work' when it is a demand around which the working class can be mobilised to fight capitalist unemployment. We are against the 'right to work' when it is a justification for scabbing.

Whenever the bourgeoisie and its media hangers-on talk about 'freedom' and the like, Marxists will always inquire 'whose freedom? Freedom to do what?' It is no coincidence that the bougeois French Revolution was fought under the banner of a set of abstractions — 'Liberty, Equality, Fraternity' — whereas the working-class Russian Revolution fought for specifics — 'Bread, Peace and Land'.

Another illustration of this point is the question of freedom of speech. The ruling class continually stress that this must be seen as a fundamental human right. In fact, it is a right which in capitalist society is subject to a thousand and one restrictions and limitations. Just try exercising it if you are a soldier, a school student, a civil servant or with your boss at work. Moreover, history has shown that the bourgeoisie are perfectly ready to dispense with any commitment to this right when they feel this is necessary to preserve their rule.

What then is the Marxist attitude to 'freedom of speech'?

In general we defend it, not because it is some divinely bestowed right, but because it is greatly to the advantage of the working class under capitalism that there should be a free flow of ideas and debate (and this will be true for people under socialism also). Indeed we make a point of defending it precisely where capitalism restricts it. What an excellent thing it would be if soldiers could freely criticise their officers, school students their teachers and workers their bosses, without fear of reprisal.

We do not, however, pretend that freedom of speech can be an absolute or universal right. We do not, for example, defend the right of the National Front to incite racial hatred or indeed to spread their Nazi ideas in any shape or form. Nor, in a workers' state, would we grant the displaced capitalist class the right to urge insurrection and counter-revolution.

But we do not make a fetish of this denial of freedom of speech, even for racists. It is not for us a matter of absolute principle to stop the mouth of every single fascist or racist regardless of circumstances, still less to ban every point of view we find obnoxious. It is always a matter of strategic and practical judgement.

But how to explain the difference between the bourgeoisie's apparent commitment to universal rights and principles and the Marxist insistence that all rights and principles are historical and dependent on circumstances? Is it a matter of hypocrisy versus honesty? Yes, but the hypocrisy and the honesty are class-based. The bourgeoisie are obliged to be hypocritical because they are a tiny minority able to rule only if they can pass their interests off as the interests of 'the whole people'.

Marxism, however, represents the working class, who are in the immense majority and therefore have no need to disguise their specific class interests. On the contrary, a clear understanding of exactly what their interests are is precisely what the working class need to achieve their freedom.

The point, however, is to change it

'The philosophers have only interpreted the world in various ways — the point is to change it.'

So runs the most famous of all Marx's quotations and, appropriately, it is carved on his gravestone in Highgate cemetery. What the quotation makes clear is that Marx was first and foremost a revolutionary whose primary concern was to participate in the overthrow of capitalism.

Yet it is also clear that Marx was very interested in 'interpreting the world'. After all, he spent the best years of his life sat in the British Museum working on an 'interpretation' of the laws of motion of capitalism. So what is the relationship between theory and practice in Marxism?

Marxism stands for the *unity* of theory and practice. Revolutionary theory is necessary for revolutionary practice. Revolutionary practice is necessary for revolutionary theory. At one moment the emphasis may be on theory, at another on practice, but in the long run, each is impossible without the other.

Let us deal first with the importance of theory for practice. The working class needs theory, its own theory, because without it it is bound to be dominated, to a greater or lesser degree, by the ideas of the bourgeoisie and the petty bourgeoisie. Everybody, consciously or unconsciously, is guided by certain general ideas about the world. If these ideas are not socialist they all inevitably turn out to be capitalist or semi-capitalist, for as Marx put it, the ruling ideas are always the ideas of the ruling class.

If workers do not believe the emancipation of the working class is the act of the working class, then they will look for salvation from above, or, worse still, come to the conclusion that no emancipation is possible at all. If workers lack a Marxist analysis of the economic crisis they will accept one or other of the various bourgeois explanations on offer: 'it's an act of god', 'it's all the fault of lazy workers' or 'powerful trade unions'. At best it's due to 'government mismanagement' and the solution is to elect a better government.

In other words, a working class not guided by Marxist theory is bound to play into the hands of its enemies.

To take two examples; in both Iran and Poland the mass of workers fought magnificently against their oppressors, but lacked any worked-out socialist theory. In both cases the gap was filled by religion. In Iran this meant the people, having overthrown one tyrant, raised another in his place, this time with the blessing of Allah. In Poland it meant the workers, and especially their leaders, were susceptible to the church's calls for peace and moderation in the face of an opponent that was preparing to strike a decisive blow.

Theory, then, is vital to effective practice. But the converse is equally true: practice is vital for the development of theory. Indeed theory derives from the problems encountered in the practical effort to change the world. It was because Marx was engaged in the struggle to change society that he needed to understand how it worked. It was because he had taken the side of the working class that he was able to analyse the workings of capitalism.

Practice is also essential as the *test* of theory. No theory, however sophisticated, can ever be a perfect representation or reflection of all the complexities of reality.

Theory is always a simplification and a generalisation. Whether it is a valid simplification depends ultimately on whether it stands the test of practice: on whether it helps or hinders humans to shape and control their world.

There have always been some would-be Marxists who have sought to separate theory and practice, to develop theory for its own sake. They have tried to achieve this without involving themselves in working-class struggles. They are destined to disappointment. They cut off theory from both its real source and from the necessary discipline of the attempt to implement it.

All the real advances in Marxist theory have come as a response to developments or problems encountered in the class struggle. Marx's pamphlet the **Civil War in France** was produced as a result of the Paris Commune, Trotsky's theory of permanent revolution from the 1905 revolution in Russia. Lenin developed his theory of imperialism in response to the First World War and wrote **State and Revolution** during the 1917 revolution.

All the outstanding figures of the Marxist tradition have been both major theorists and active revolutionaries. Theory is essential, but our aim is the unity of theory and practice *in practice*. The point, as was said at the start, is to change the world.

Chapter Four:
Strategies of the system

'You socialists would abolish democracy . . .'

ONE OF the main charges made against Marxism by the ruling class and by reformists is that it is anti-democratic. Thus Labour Party leaders often describe themselves as *democratic* socialists in opposition to Marxists. Partly this is based on the experiences of Stalinism, but also it's because Marxists advocate revolution.

Revolution, they argue, would be against the rule of parliament and for them parliament is synonymous with democracy. They're right, of course. Revolution cannot come through parliament, and indeed revolution would overthrow parliament. But they are quite wrong to identify parliament with democracy.

In reality the democracy offered by a capitalist parliament is always extraordinarily limited. Firstly, parliamentary democracy offers no means by which electors can control their representatives. Once elected there is nothing to stop MPs breaking all their pre-election promises. Secondly, MPs do not, in practice, control government. Rather it is the government through a mixture of patronage and pressure that controls the MPs. Thirdly, the government does not control the decisive area of society, namely the economy, which remains in the hands of big business.

Finally, it must be remembered that apart from parliament almost every important institution in society is run without any democracy whatsoever. In the police, the army, in every industry and business (private or nationalised), in the civil service, the schools and colleges, the hospitals, the mass media and so on, the principle of administration is the same — authoritarian appointment from above. In all those areas democratic decisions are never even considered.

In short, the idea that parliament equals democracy, the 'rule of the people', is nonsense. It is little more than a democratic fig leaf covering the nakedness of capitalist rule. What's more, as the example of Chile proved for the umpteenth time — where in 1973 the elected governent of Salvador Allende was overthrown by the army with the most horrific bloodshed and repression — 'parliamentary democracy' is a fig leaf the ruling class is always willing to dispense with if it interferes with their vital interests.

In contrast, workers' revolution would produce a society far more democratic in every way than any bourgeois democracy. It would begin by destroying the capitalist state and establishing a new state of workers' councils. These would be made up of delegates from workplaces, where collective discussion would take place, and who would thus be accountable to, and recallable by, those who elected them. The undemocratic and authoritarian armed forces and police would be replaced by democratically controlled workers' militia responsible to the workers' councils. This workers' power would then be used to establish the foundation of real 'rule by the people' — the social ownership and control of the means of production.

Whatever the political set-up, ultimate power in any society rests with those who control the decisive forces of production. Unless these are controlled by the working class all talk of democracy remains a sham.

Furthermore, Marxists not only advocate workers' democracy in the future, but also fight to defend and extend it in the present. We defend all those democratic rights won by struggle in the past — the right to vote, to strike, to independent trade unions, to free speech — against all attempts by the ruling class to restrict or remove them. We stand for the equal application of those rights to all workers regardless of race, nationality or sex. In all this Marxists are consistent democrats.

Isn't the state neutral?

When the police arrest you on a picket line they are not 'interfering in politics', merely 'maintaining public order'. When the judge or magistrate sentences you he is not interested in the politics of the case, only in 'upholding the law'. The armed forces, likewise, are 'outside politics', they merely 'defend the nation' in the Falklands, 'keep the peace' in Belfast, and 'maintain essential services' when they scab on strikes.

Senior civil servants are non-political too, they simply follow instructions from the government, which, in turn, exercises its power 'in the national interest'. Over the lot stands the Queen. She is 'above' politics, symbolising the unity of the nation.

So run the myths of the ruling class about its state. They reflect a theory of the state developed over centuries by the bourgeoisie. It contains two central ideas. First that the state represents the interests of *society as a whole*, it is above class. Second, that it is indispensable; without it society would disintegrate into a war of all against all, because ordinary people are 'naturally' bad/greedy/stupid, and so need to be ruled.

Marx rejected this view root and branch. He argued that society would disintegrate without a state not because of people's natural inadequacies but because society is divided into classes with conflicting interests. Societies existed for thousands of years without any state apparatus because classes had not yet emerged. Similarly, after class divisions have been abolished a state will no longer be needed. Public order in a classless society will be kept simply by organisations of the general public without any need for 'armed bodies of men' standing over society. The very existence of the state testifies to class antagonisms.

Consequently the state is anything but non-political, rather it is the essence of political power. It is *never* the representative of the people 'as a whole', but *always* an instrument through which one class maintains its rule over other classes.

The existence of parliamentary democracy doesn't change this, for every state rests ultimately on economic foundations.

Police, judges, soldiers, are not themselves productive; they and their activities have to be paid for. So, in the final analysis, it is always the class that controls the economy that controls the state. Usually the ruling class exercises this control directly by ensuring that senior positions in the state are held by loyal members of its own class. (Thus in Britain today more than 80 per cent of judges and generals went to public school.) But even when sections of the state pass into other hands, as in Nazi Germany, the ruling class can still use its economic power to make sure the state protects its interests (German big business did very well under Hitler).

Because of this, the old reformist idea that by winning a majority in parliament, the state can be taken over and used for socialist purposes, is a complete pipe dream. Faced with a reforming government whose policies represent a challenge to capitalist priorities the state machine — acting in concert with big business — has immense resources of obstructions and pressure. Should the government resist those pressures (a highly unlikely event where the Labour Party is concerned) it can still resort to direct force, as the Chilean state did ten years ago.

The working class cannot 'take over' the bourgeois state; it must smash it. This is the central conclusion of the theory of the state developed by Marx and Engels and re-emphasised by Lenin in his great book **The State and Revolution**. Smashing the state means disbanding the police, sacking the judges, breaking the bourgeois army by winning the rank and file over to the workers, and removing the bureaucratic ministries of Whitehall. Above all it involves completely replacing the old state apparatus with a new apparatus arising directly from working-class struggle.

Whose law and whose order?

The Tory Party is the enthusiastic party of law and order. Everyone must obey the law they say, because it is the law that makes civilisation possible. The law, they claim, protects society as a whole, and individuals within it, from the threat posed by a minority of anti-social elements. Conjuring up their favourite image of the 'grannie mugged by thugs', they go so far as to proclaim that the law protects the weak from the strong.

The Labour right shares this view, except for arguing that their own 'moderate' and 'reasonable' policies would make the maintenance of law and order easier. The Labour lefts are slightly more sceptical. Where they consider a law to be especially bad (for example anti-union laws) or a cause especially important (such as the Campaign for Nuclear Disarmament) they sometimes argue that breaking the law is justified. But fundamentally they go along with the right in accepting the overall framework of the law as it stands.

The Marxist view of the law however *is* different. It sees the law as defending not society in general, or people in general, but the existing system of society, namely capitalism. Contemporary law is, first and foremost, a set of rules requiring behaviour appropriate to the smooth running of a capitalist economy. Since a capitalist economy necessarily produces a society dominated by a capitalist class, the law necessarily defends the interests of that class.

One reason — in addition to the constant flow of law and order propaganda — why the right-wing view retains a certain plausibility is that most people take the capitalist functioning of the law more or less for granted. They are so used to it that they regard it as 'natural'. But consider what would happen if the law didn't reflect and reinforce the property relations of capitalism. What if, for example, it was illegal to charge interest on money loaned? What if judges were in the habit of ruling that millionaires riding around in Rolls-Royces in broad daylight were asking to be robbed, in the same way they suggest that women on their own at night are asking to be raped? Or even more fundamentally, what if the law prohibited the sale of labour power in the same way it does the sale of children? Clearly if the law were changed in any of these ways the capitalist system would break down within weeks if not days.

Not surprisingly the administration of the law reflects its inherent class character. The ruling class retains a firm grip on the higher echelons of the legal profession. About 80 per cent of judges were educated at public schools, and it is still extremely difficult to become a barrister without private means. Anyone who has observed court proceedings at any level cannot fail to notice that they consist overwhelmingly of the middle and upper classes sitting in judgement on the working classes.

These facts give the lie to another cherished myth about British justice — the alleged 'independence of the judiciary from politics'. Now judges *are* often independent from *parliament*. Given that parliament is an elected institution this is actually an advantage for the ruling class. It means that should the 'wrong' people get elected to parliament, and should these people by some mischance pass some inconvenient legislation, the judges will always be there to come up with an 'interpretation' of the law that sets matters right again. It means that should the right wing decide that parliamentary democracy itself is inconvenient then there are some judges around to provide a legal rubber stamp for the counter-revolutionary activities of the generals and police chiefs.

The real function of the law therefore is the opposite of that claimed by the right. Far from protecting civilisation it protects a social order that threatens the existence of any civilisation. Far from protecting the weak from the strong it protects the rich from the poor, the exploiters from the exploited, the powerful from the potentially powerful. Any movement for serious social change cannot fail to come into conflict with the law. If it has illusions about it, it is hamstrung from the beginning.

So how do they maintain their rule?

All ruling classes maintain their rule by a combination of force and persuasion. These two aspects of ruling-class power always complement and reinforce each other. In the middle ages the feudal lord had his soldiers to ensure the peasants performed their work and paid their taxes and the Catholic church to explain to them that the feudal order was God's order. If the peasants rebelled, the church was on hand to condemn their revolt as sinful. If anyone questioned the teachings of the church, the soldiers were on hand to burn them as heretics.

Today the ruling class has the police — and ultimately the army — to arrest pickets and demonstrators, and the mass media to explain that pickets and demonstrators are extremist monsters who threaten 'civilisation as we know it'. In so far as the media is successful with its propaganda, it is easier for the police to smash picket lines. Equally, every success of the police in breaking a picket line reinforces the central message of ruling-class ideology, that working people are powerless.

The use of these two methods of control is something that does not change. It is a feature of all class-divided society. The fundamental antagonism between the classes is such that no ruling class is ever able to rule purely by consent. On the other hand, the fact that the exploited and the 'have-nots' always vastly outnumber the exploiters and the 'haves' means that no ruling class can survive purely by force.

What does change — and sometimes very dramatically — is the balance between repression and ideological control. In some cases, such as South Africa, it is clear that the existing regime has lost practically all legitimacy and credibility in the eyes of the majority of the population and therefore has to depend primarily on force. In comparison, in Britain and Western Europe the element of force, though undoubtedly increasing in recent years, is still a secondary factor. The existing political and economic order — though not necessarily the particular government — still retains the support of the large majority.

One of the most important features of bourgeois rule in modern capitalism is that simple ruling-class manipulation of the education system and the mass media is insufficient to maintain ideological control. The size, strength and organisation of the working class is too great, and the daily clash of interests at the point of production too all-pervasive, for straightforward capitalist propaganda to be enough. Besides, propaganda may be powerful but there is a limit to the extent to which it can get people to believe things that run directly counter to their own experience.

Consequently, the crucial role in the stabilisation of advanced capitalism is played by institutions which have their base not in the ruling class but in the working class, and which are seen as expressing working-class interests and working-class opposition to the system's worst excesses. Nonetheless, they accept and purvey the basic premises of the system and thereby serve to integrate the working class within it.

In Britain this role is played primarily by the trade union bureaucracy and the Labour Party. If one looks at the strategy of the British ruling class in this light, it is clear that over the last quarter of a century it has pursued one single, central aim — that of raising the rate of profit of British capital — but has done so by different means. Essentially, it has oscillated between a strategy with the balance tilted towards force and one with the balance tilted towards consent.

In the former strategy the ruling class relies principally on its own party — the Tories — and on the law, the police and the willingness of employers to take on the trade unions, combined with an economic policy that stresses market forces and encourages unemployment to rise. It attempts to impose cuts in working-class living stndards and weaken trade union resistance by more or less frontal assault. This has been the dominant approach in the Thatcher years.

In the latter strategy it relies principally on the trade union bureaucracy. It attempts to reach an accommodation with the trade union leaders so that they in turn will sell the deal to their rank and file and impose the necessary discipline to make it stick. This was the approach of the Social Contract made between the trade union leaders and the Labour governments of Harold Wilson and James Callaghan in the 1970s.

As one strategy fails, so the ruling class switches its allegiance to the other.

Divided we fall . . .

'Ye are many — they are few', wrote the poet Shelley in 1819, when urging the workers to 'rise like lions' against their oppressors. It was true then and it remains true today. The ruling class proper — the big shareholders and financiers, the holders of key posts in industry, the City and the state — is tiny, amounting to only one or two per cent of the population. How then does this small minority of exploiters maintain its power over the vast majority of exploited?

Clearly part of the answer is through the use of direct force — such as the massive police operation against the miners in the 1984-5 strike. Equally clearly another part of the answer lies in the ruling class's control of the media and the education system, which enables it to indoctrinate much of the working class with capitalist reactionary ideas.

However, both these mechanisms of control — the head-bashing and the head-fixing — are made easier and more effective by the divisions which exist within the working class — divisions of craft, locality, nationality, race, sex and so on. Let's take two examples of how this works.

First the division between British workers and Irish workers. The view that the Irish are stupid (perpetually reinforced in innumerable non-jokes by innumerable non-comedians), and that the war in Northern Ireland is an incomprehensible conflict between religious maniacs, has permitted the army and police to develop there techniques of repression (such as snatch squads) which if first used in Britain would have provoked a chorus of liberal protest. Once perfected and accepted these techniques can then be transferred to Britain for use against workers here with relative impunity.

Second, the division between men and women. The traditional stereotype of the working-class woman as housewife and mother who leaves the world of work, trade unionism, and politics to her husband gives the working-class man a position of relative privilege and dominance in the home. But immediately a strike or dispute breaks out this dubious advantage backfires. The wife, if previously uninvolved and uninformed, experiences the strike not as a positive collective struggle but as a loss of family income, and so as a threat to the security of the home. She is therefore vulnerable to the mass media's anti-strike propaganda.

What then is the root of these many divisions and how can they be overcome? The root lies in the nature of capitalism itself. Capitalism is a system based on competition between independent producing units, be they small shops, giant multinational companies or even capitalist states. And this competition, Marx pointed out, 'separates individuals one from another, not only the bourgeois but still more the workers, in spite of the fact that it brings them together'.

Under capitalism labour power becomes a commodity which every worker has to sell to live. This makes every other worker a potential competitor in the labour market, and so long as workers see each other as competitors they are prey to every prejudice about their rivals — the Japanese, German, Korean, black, women — workers who are supposed to be 'taking their jobs'. And obviously the ruling class does everything it can to foster these prejudices.

But if the divisions derive from the nature of capitalism it is only in the course of struggle that they can be overcome. Clearly socialists must oppose all divisions in the working class at all times, exposing their consequences. However, socialist propaganda by itself cannot defeat the propaganda of the system. Only when it connects with workers' actual experience in struggle can it be really effective.

The best illustration of this is the question of racism. This is one of the deepest divisions in the working class, and at present most white workers are to some extent racist, not violently racist like the National Front, but racist nevertheless. Moreover it is a racism which is highly resistant to any amount of well-intentioned liberal moralising.

But consider what happens when black and white workers find themselves on strike together and on the same picket line. At once there is created the bond of being in the same struggle against the same enemy. The argument about class unity as opposed to racial division becomes concrete — it fits the immediate situation. When strike-breakers approach, either the white workers overcome their prejudices and link arms with their black workmates, or they hand an obvious present to the boss. Thus the class is unified in struggle.

Of course divisions are not always overcome and often workers are defeated because of them. But this we can say: the moment of the working class's unification will coincide with the moment of its victory for the very simple reason that 'We are many and they are few'.

Chapter Five:
What do socialists say about . . . ?

Overpopulation

ONE OF THE most common explanations of the scenes of mass starvation in Ethiopia and of the appalling phenomenon of third world poverty is that these countries suffer from 'overpopulation'. There are simply too many mouths to feed, or so it is said.

This argument is given added force by the fact that it seems to be believed by a number of third world governments. In recent years, for example, there have been the late Sanjay Gandhi's forcible sterilisation campaign in India, and the one-child policy in 'communist' China.

Nevertheless despite this powerful backing it is an argument that cannot withstand the slightest contact with the facts. Let us begin with the example of Ethiopia itself. Ethiopia has a population of 31 million in an area of 1,222,000 square kilometres (five times the size of the UK). This gives it a population density of 25 per square kilometre, as compared with 228 per square kilometre in Britain. Comparisons could also be made with West Germany (population density 248 per square kilometre), the Netherlands (347), and Japan (315). In other words, far from being 'overpopulated', Ethiopia is, in reality, very sparsely populated.

But perhaps Ethiopia is an exception, or perhaps it is unreasonable to compare a largely rural third world country with advanced industrial nations. Let us have a look at a number of third world countries.

First of all the large majority of third world countries have relatively low population densities. Not that this helps them much. For example, Chad, the Congo, Sudan, Somalia, Mali, Paraguay and Bolivia all have population densities of less than 10 per square kilometre, yet all remain desperately poor.

But what of India and China with their so-called 'teeming millions' and their attempts at state population control? In fact, both have a population density less than Britain — India 208 per square kilometre, and China 102.

Finally, there are those areas of the third world that are densely populated: Bangladesh (616 per square kilometre), Hong Kong (4,827), Singapore (4,122), South Korea (382), Taiwan (486), Mauritius (480). Strangely — at least strangely for the 'overpopulation' theory — many of these areas turn out to be among the most prosperous anywhere in the third world. Hong Kong, Singapore and Taiwan are, after Japan, the three richest places in the whole of southern and eastern Asia, with South Korea making rapid progress in the same direction. Mauritius, off the east coast of Africa, is undoubtedly poor, but it has wealth per head more than four times the average for the area.

In short, an examination of the facts shows that there is absolutely no causal connection between high population and poverty. Nor should this be surprising, for it is a question not only of facts but also of simple logic. Every extra person is not only an extra mouth to feed, but also an extra worker to produce goods.

Also, it is important to ask *why* the poplation is growing in third world countries. The answer is not that people are having more children — the birth rate for the third world as a whole is 33 per thousand per year, slightly less than it was in Britain until the end of the 19th century — but that the death rate, in particular the infant mortality rate, is falling. This in turn comes from an improvement, albeit slight, in general living standards (diet, medical care, sanitation and so on). Far from population growth causing poverty, it is in general a result of a small increase in prosperity.

Why then, if it is such nonsense, is the overpopulation argument so popular? The answer is simple. It is because, for the world's ruling classes in both the developed countries and the third world itself, it is the perfect alibi. It distracts attention from the vast sums spent on arms which, if redirected, could solve the world's malnutrition problem, from the obscenity of 'food mountains' hoarded because there is no profit in selling to the poor, and from the looting of the third world by imperialism and the multinationals. Like so many capitalist ideas it shifts the blame for the results of oppression from the system onto the oppressed themselves.

The myth of overpopulation can be compared to society's other myths. For example that 'people are unemployed because they're too lazy to work'; that women are raped and battered 'because they ask for it'; that people are poor because they are idle and spendthrift.

The origins of the whole 'overpopulation' theory date back to the 18th-century parson and economist, Thomas Malthus, whose 'Essay on Population', published in 1798, was designed to counter radical ideas coming from the French Revolution. Marx scathingly dismissed Malthus' theory as 'a libel on the human race'. 186 years have not improved it.

Religion

'Criticism of religion,' wrote the young Marx, 'is the foundation of all criticism', and when he wrote this, in Germany in 1843, it was certainly true. At that time society and social thought were very much dominated by religion.

Today in Britain the criticism of religion may seem a much less urgent matter. However a glance round the world, at countries as different as Poland, Iran, Ireland, and Nicaragua, reveals many instances of religion exerting a major influence on the course of the class struggle. It is not, therefore, a question Marxists can afford to forget or ignore.

What, then, is the Marxist attitude to religion? Consistent Marxists are, of course, atheists. The Marxist outlook is materialist. It regards the ideas in people's heads, including religious ideas, as a response to the material conditions of their lives. As Marx put it, 'Man makes religion, religion does not make man.' For Marx religion is an upside-down world view produced by an upside-down world. People deprived by class society of control of their own labour and the product of that labour are thereby deprived of control of their lives and of their society. They respond by projecting their aspirations to control their own destiny on to a supernatural omnipotent god, by projecting their dreams of happiness, peace and fulfillment on to an imaginary afterlife.

Religion arose first in circumstances where the low level of the productive forces made starvation, suffering and alienation inevitable. It gave illusory hope to those whose real situation was hopeless. It was, in Marx's words, 'The sigh of the oppressed creature, the heart of a heartless world . . . the opium of the people'.

Arising in this way, religion also serves to reinforce the conditions which generate it. Now that these conditions are no longer inevitable, it impedes the struggle to control the bakery on earth by promising 'pie in the sky' hereafter. Religion therefore becomes a weapon in the hands of the ruling class. It sanctifies their laws as god's laws, their order as god's order, and their wars as god's wars. In preaching submission to divine authority it simultaneously encourages submission to worldly power.

For Marxists, the struggle against religious illusions is a necessary part of the struggle against the social system that produces those illusions. But in seeking to combat the influence of religion we should not oversimplify its political role. Religion is not always the straightforward ally of all reaction. It can only sustain the class society on which it rests if it retains its hold on the minds of the masses. It therefore has to be adaptable, move with the times, proclaim its sympathy with the poor and even at times for popular movements. Thus the Catholic church in Poland could only exercise its moderating influence on Solidarity if it presented itself as an ally of the workers' movement.

Because religion is 'the sigh of the oppressed creature' as well as the 'opium of the people', and because the consciousness of the oppressed has been dominated by religion for centuries, it is often the case that genuine popular movements assume a religious form.

This is particularly the case where the influence of Marxism is weak and where the peasantry plays the major role. It is in these cases that religion assumes its most radical form.

Obviously Marxists should not confuse the religious illusions of the oppressed with the established churches of the oppressors, any more than we confuse the reformist illusions of workers with the reformism of right-wing politicians. The drug addict is not the same as the drugs racketeer. Nor do we use these religious illusions (as the Stalinists did over Poland) to refuse solidarity with those in struggle.

Nonetheless, even in its most left-wing forms religion remains an obstacle to the self-emancipation of the working class, always opening the way to notions of class peace and reconciliation. Above all it cannot provide the scientific understanding of society which is the precondition of transforming society. Only Marxism can do that.

War

The rise of the anti-nuclear movement has brought with it a resurgence of pacifism. Marxists, of course, support all movements to disarm the bourgeois state and share with the pacifists the desire to put an end to war and violence. The creation of a society totally free from war is in fact one of our central aims.

But Marxists are not pacifists. Indeed, we are *opposed* to pacifism.

The first reason for this is that pacifism is completely ineffective as an instrument for preventing or resisting war. This has been proved time and again in the twentieth century.

Both the First and the Second World Wars were preceded by widespread pacifist moods and powerful pacifist movements. A form of pacifism was the dominant ideology of the majority of the Second International, which organised millions of workers before 1914. And in the 1930s pacifist hopes were concentrated in the League of Nations. In both cases these pacifist movements not only failed to stop the war, but also collapsed into total impotence once the wars began.

The root of pacifism's weakness lies in its failure to diagnose the causes of war. Pacifism tends to regard war as simply the product of misguided violent people with misguided violent attitudes. It therefore sees the remedy as lying in the large-scale conversion of people to peaceful attitudes. In reality war has much deeper roots. Its main cause in the modern world is the capitalist system, which subordinates all production, and with it the whole of society, to the struggle for capital accumulation, which by its very nature is competitive.

If the oubreak of violence between individual capitalists is prevented by the existence of the capitalist state, which has a monopoly of armed force, the existence of many such states only makes war between them all the more inevitable. Moreover, the power of the capitalist state is such that it can impose war on its population regardless of whether they want it or not, just as Thatcher can site Cruise missiles in Britain regardless of the opinion polls.

So even if pacifism succeeded in converting a huge majority to 'non-violence' it would still not be able to prevent war. The only way to abolish war is to abolish the system that generates it, and replace competitive production for profit by collective, co-operative, production for need. And this brings us to the second reason why Marxists are opposed to pacifism.

In the struggle to change society, pacifism is not only ineffective, it is positively reactionary. Pacifism preaches non-violence equally to all classes in society, but the only class it has any chance of influencing (apart from the petty bourgeoisie where it generally originates) are the oppressed. The prospect of converting the ruling classes of the world, who know perfectly well that their wealth and power has always rested on the use of violence, is as remote as the prospect of the second coming.

Apply this to such situations as Nicaragua, Vietnam or South Africa. Unless one hopes for the pacifist conversion of the likes of Somoza, Nixon, Reagan, Botha and others, what pacifism would actually mean is telling the Nicaraguans, Vietnamese and black South Africans they mustn't resist imperialism, genocide and apartheid because that would involve 'violence'.

Pacifism therefore disarms the oppressed in the face of capitalist and imperialist repression. It's exactly the same where the class struggle is concerned.

Finally, pacifism paints capitalism in far more rosy colours than it deserves. By counterposing the struggle for peace to the struggle for socialism pacifism encourages the idea that there could be a violence-free, war-free capitalism. This can only play into the hands of the cynical politicians, both bourgeois and reformist, who have much experience in deceiving the working class with hypocritical rhetoric about peace, while preparing to plunge them into war.

Marxists see the pre-eminent divisions of the world not as those between nations, but between classes. Workers have nothing to gain from the waging of war between their capitalist rulers, except hardship, suffering, and death. Nor will they gain by victory in war — since this only strengthens the ruling class, the better to exploit the workers. As internationalists, Marxists call on workers of all countries to unite. In the case of an imperialist war between nations, we would call on workers of both countries to oppose the war and work for the defeat and overthrow of their own ruling class.

Terrorism

Marxism equals revolution. Revolution equals violence. Violence equals terrorism. Therefore Marxism equals terrorism. This line of argument is repeatedly insinsuated by the ruling class and the media. However, the mainstream of the Marxist tradition has always been strongly opposed to the use of terrorism.

The matter was first fully debated in Russia at the end of the nineteenth century when the Narodniks — or 'Friends of the people' — were waging terrorist campaigns in their struggle against tsarism. At that time the leading figures of the Russian Marxist movement — Lenin, Plekhanov, Trotsky and others — came out firmly against terrorism and that has remained the position of our movement ever since.

The exploitation and oppression that we are fighting against are the products not of particular government ministers, or even particular governments, but of the world economic system of capitalism. They can be ended only by the overthrow of this system and that requires mass action by many millions of workers, not the assassination of individuals or the blowing up of particular targets, whatever their nature. Equally the society which we want to put in the place of capitalism, one in which working people own and control industry and the state, can only be created by the *mass* activity of workers themselves, not the actions of a minority.

Terrorism, whatever its subjective motive, represents an attempt by a tiny minority to substitute themselves for this mass action, to do for the working class what the working class can only do for itself.

Even where the terrorist forces are large, the very nature of the enterprise obliges them to operate independently of and behind the back of the working class. And even when terrorism has mass support, it cannot help but encourage in those masses an attitude of passivity, an expectation of liberation from above.

Additionally, terrorism, if it results in the loss of innocent lives, alienates working-class people from causes they might otherwise be won to support. In so doing it creates a favourable atmosphere for increased state repression, which can be, and will be, directed against the left and the workers' movement in general. Finally, it frequently destroys or wastes the lives of many ardent young revolutionaries.

Terrorism, therefore, is not a weapon of struggle of the working class, but of other classes. Trotsky once described the terrorist as 'a liberal with a bomb'.

Although some deluded would-be Marxists or anarchists (the Baader-Meinhof group, the Italian Red Brigades for instance) have turned to terrorism, it is the middle-class-led nationalist or communal movement that is most characteristic of terrorist organisation. It is therefore no surprise that terrorism should now be rampant in the Lebanon, where there exist a number of national and religious communities all driven to utter desperation by a veritable avalanche of oppression, while at the same time there is no socialist or working-class alternative even in sight.

But Marxist criticism of terrorism has nothing in common with the hypocritical condemnations and denunciations issued ceaselessly by the ruling-class politicians and the media. When it comes to violence and the slaughter of innocents, the likes of Reagan and Thatcher can and do commit worse atrocities than the most extreme terrorists. In any conflict between the forces of the imperialist or capitalist states and the terrorist who represents the oppressed, our sympathies are unreservedly with the terrorist.

Nor do we accept the alternative which the bourgeois politicians counterpose to terrorism, namely passive aquiescence to oppression or, at best, a vote in parliamentary elections.

From the Marxist viewpoint, parliamentary democracy suffers from the same basic flaw as terrorism — it is a matter of expecting a small elite, albeit MPs instead of gunmen, to act on behalf of the workers themselves. The ballot and the bomb are at bottom two sides of the substitutionist coin.

We do not deny to the working class and the oppressed the right to use violence against their oppressors. On the contrary, we think such violence is unavoidable because the ruling classes of the world will not surrender their power and privileges without a bitter struggle. We simply insist that, to achieve its aims, such violence must be exercised not by small elites, but by the mass of the working class, and directed not against individuals, but against the roots of the capitalist system.

Class

The term 'class' is commonly used in a loose and confused way to refer to such things as a person's family background, education and social standing. Sociologists also employ class as a category in surveys. Usually they regard a person's class as being defined by their occupation, with occupations ranked in five or six 'classes' according to their supposed social status. In both its 'everyday' and sociological usage, the purpose of the concept is to serve as a convenient label which can be attached to individuals so as to give some general idea of their 'life-style' and attitudes.

For Marxists, the concept of class serves a very different

purpose. Its aim is not to determine the appropriate label for every individual, nor to depict exactly every gradation and shading of the social hierarchy. It is to identify the fundamental social forces whose conflict is the driving force of history.

The Marxist theory of class is therefore, first and foremost, a *theory of class struggle*.

What makes an aggregate of individuals into a 'class' is not that they all have the same 'life-style' or attitudes, or that they all receive the same pay, but that they have certain basic common interests in opposition to the interests of another class or classes. It is this conflict of interests that generates class struggle.

There are of course innumerable conflicts of interests in society, ranging from the trivial squabble between neighbours to the tragic conflicts betwen people of different races or nations. But what makes class conflict more fundamental than all these other divisions is that it concerns conflicts of interest *in the process of production* — that is, in the very basis of society, in the starting point of all historical development.

Antagonistic interests in the process of production are the result of exploitation, that is the extraction by one group of people of *surplus* from the labour of another group. It is exploitation that divides society into opposed classes. The key to exploitation is the effective possession (ownership or control) of the major means of production by one social group to the exclusion of the other group, who are thereby forced to work for the dominant group and to yield to them control of the social surplus.

Historically these exploitative relations of production have taken many forms and have given rise to different sets of opposed classes, such as slave owners and slaves, lords and serfs, landowners and peasants.

In capitalist society the class struggle is principally between the capitalists (those who own and control capital) and the working class (those who live by the sale of their labour power).

It is now nearly 140 years since Marx advanced the view that this is the fundamental division in modern society. Since then sociologists (the main bourgeois ideologists in this field) have never ceased to claim that changes in the class structures of capitalism have refuted Marx's proposition and made it 'out of date'. In particular they have argued that as capitalism develops so the working class declines as a proportion of society while the middle class expands. Recently this old bourgeois argument has been given a new lease of life by certain well-known 'Marxists' such as Eric Hobsbawm and André Gorz.

In fact the argument rests entirely on the notion of class as a matter of attitudes, lifestyle and occupational category. The vast majority of those claimed for the expanding 'middle class' — clerical and office workers, shop assistants, health workers (including nurses), teachers and the like — are, in terms of the relations of production, clearly workers. They neither own nor control the means of production. They live entirely by the sale of their labour power, and they are exploited by capital. They share the same basic economic interests as miners and carworkers, dockers and factory workers.

There are indeed intermediate layers (the 'middle classes') — managers and administrators — who are not themselves big capitalists, but who have some control over the means of production and who also direct the labour of others. But these remain relatively few in number. In terms of shaping history, it is not this layer that is decisive. The fundamental division and the fundamental struggle is now, more than ever, between capital and labour.

Crime

The capitalist class has a love-hate relationship with crime, as can be seen from a glance at the capitalist media. The newspapers dutifully condemn crime but they also delight in crime stories. 'Sex Monster', 'The Beast' and 'Crime Rate Soars' are among Fleet Street's favourite headlines. TV and films are the same. There must be a thousand cops and robbers shows for every film or play dealing with a strike (the capitalists are unequivocally opposed to strikes).

Nor is this just a matter of boosting sales and chasing ratings. The ambivalence reflects deep-rooted class interests.

On the one hand the ruling class is officially, and in a sense genuinely, opposed to crime. It needs the 'rule of law' to prevent the poor helping themselves to the property of the rich, who do not appreciate being arbitrarily deprived of their Rolls-Royces and diamond tiaras, even if they are insured. Moreover, the smooth running of capitalism requires a degree of order in its business transactions, though this does not prevent numerous capitalists and capitalist officials committing all sorts of crimes.

On the other hand, the ruling class knows that crime does not really threaten it — a class *cannot* be dispossessed by any number of individual robberies — and it knows that it reaps considerable benefits from the existence of crime. Every time the state is seen to deal with a crime it reinforces its claims to represent the general good of society against anti-social elements — to be the defender of the weak against the strong — and masks its essential function of defending the rich against the poor.

There is nothing like a real or imaginary crime wave for giving the state an excuse to strengthen its repressive powers. There is nothing like the 'law-and-order' issue for electing right-wing governments and putting 'moderates' on the defensive. For the capitalists, crime plays the same role as the external 'enemy'. If crime did not exist it would be necessary to invent it.

Anyway the capitalist system produces crime like running produces sweat. An economy based on competition, greed, exploitation and alienation cannot do otherwise. Engels summed up the matter in a speech in 1845. 'Present day society,' he said, 'which breeds hostility between the individual man and everyone else, thus produces a social war of all against all which inevitably in individual cases assumes a brutal, barbarously violent form — that of crime.'

Consequently, all those politicians' speeches promising a crackdown on crime are so much hot air. Capitalist governments can no more end crime than they can end capitalism.

But what of socialism? In the speech quoted above Engels also maintained that a socialist society would 'put an axe to the root of crime'. To many this might seem a far-fetched claim. But provided we understand by 'socialism' what Marx and Engels understood by it, and don't confuse it with Russian-type state capitalism masquerading as socialism, then it is not hard to see how crime could be abolished.

A fully socialist society, in the Marxist sense, would be a society in which there was an abundance of the necessities of life (this is quite within reach of modern technology), and in which goods were distributed according to need — that is, truly equally. In such a society, economic crime would become progressively pointless and impossible.

Assume, for example, that everyone wanting a car could have one supplied free and that all cars were designed for use, not prestige or status. There would then be no reason to steal cars — they couldn't be sold — and if some eccentric wanted to accumulate cars for personal use it would both be glaringly obvious and not matter much. Alternatively, assume that cars are discontinued and that instead there is a free and comprehensive public transport system which takes everyone wherever they want to go. Again, the opportunity and motive for crime would disappear.

Socialism would mean that eventually all goods and services would be put on this kind of footing.

This leaves crimes against the person, committed not from economic motives but from anger, passion, jealousy, bitterness — crimes such as murder, rape and assault. Even today these are only a tiny proportion of crimes and they too have social roots — roots socialism will put an axe to.

At present one of the main causes and arenas of such crime is the restrictive capitalist family, which binds people — through social pressure and economic dependency — in relationships they find intolerable. Socialism will abolish this oppressive family by spreading the responsibility for childcare and housework and cutting all ties of dependency. People will be free to live, or not live, with who they want. In fact socialism will humanise and liberate all personal relationships. This cannot help, at the very least, but greatly reduce all crimes against the person.

The conclusion is simple. The only real fight against crime is the fight against capitalism — itself, the biggest crime of all.

The family

Conservative politicians of all parties never cease singing the praises of 'the family'. This phenomenon reflects the fact that 'Defend the family' has always been a key slogan and rallying cry for the ruling class. In view of these people's attitudes to such things as child benefit, cuts in education, health and social services, housing provision and the rest, all this pro-family propaganda could easily be dismissed as just monstrous hypocrisy.

Nevertheless it is important to recognise that there is an element of sincere class interest involved here. The ruling class recognises, and has always recognised, that the family is a deeply conservative institution. They know that in so far as they can get working-class men and above all working-class women to view the world exclusively from the perspective of their individual family unit they can create a powerful counterweight to class identification and class consciousness. They know that 'protecting my family' was ever the alibi of the scab; that in so far as women remain mentally imprisoned in the home (even when they do go out to work) they will not develop a perspective of changing society; and that 99 times out of 100 the first authority confronted by the young rebel and revolutionary is the authority of the family.

Consequently the ruling class has carefully nurtured a mythology of the family. This mythology has two main elements. First, the family is projected as a universal, eternal, unchanging institution reflecting fixed biological and psychological drives. The family is 'normal'; the family is a matter of human nature. Anyone not living within the accepted family structure or challenging this structure (by being gay, for example) is therefore labelled 'abnormal', 'unnatural' and 'deviant'.

Secondly, the family is presented as an idyllic haven of harmony, love and security; an institution which is perfectly adapted to the needs of both society and the individual. Anyone outside the family is therefore not only 'abnormal' but also 'deprived'.

Marxism rejects this reactionary nonsense. The family is not a natural but a social institution. Like any other social institution it has historical origins, roughly coinciding with the emergence of private property and the division of society into classes between five and ten thousand years ago. It has since undergone a long process of historical development in which it has assumed widely differing forms.

The result of this development is that the contemporary nuclear family is a structure adapted primarily not to the needs of men, women and children but to the needs of a particular form of society, namely capitalism, and to its overriding aim, the accumulation of capital.

In the capitalist class it is a mechanism for the maintenance and inheritance of private property and class position. In the working class it serves to produce and reproduce supplies of proficient labour power at very little cost to the employers or their state.

This makes the reality of family life (in all social classes but especially the working class) bear little or no relation to the idealised image. On the contrary, the family constitutes a major arena of oppression in which innumerable unhappy couples are bound together by economic and social dependence; in which half the working class, women, are confined and confirmed in the socially subordinate role of housewife.

The family is also, far more often than is generally acknowledged, an arena of appalling physical and psychological violence, of wife beating and child battering, of father-daughter rape, of repression, inhibition and victimisation of its own members.

Of course, despite this most people still do choose to live in families. The social pressures on them to do so are considerable and the alternative under capitalism can be grim — loneliness and isolation in most cases.

This brings us to the Marxist attitude to the family in the future. Marxists are opposed to the family as it is presently constituted. But the family cannot be banned or simply abolished. It must be replaced and what replaces it must be experienced by the vast majority as something better, more liberating and more fulfilling.

This involves complete equal pay and job opportunities for women in a context of full employment. It involves socialising the burden of housework by means of good communal restaurants and laundries in every neighbourhood. It involves sharing childcare through nursery places for all children. It involves a lot of other far-reaching changes in the organisation of society. So far-reaching, indeed, that they are inconceivable without a total transformation of society, a social revolution.

Chapter Six:
The shape of the world

Surely we must defend the national interest?

FROM THE cradle to the grave we're encouraged to think of ourselves as members of a nation. Whether it is the World Cup or a royal wedding, the school history lesson or the latest export figures, the pressure is the same — identify with Britain, back Britain, believe Britain is best. And of course the same thing is going on in every other country. Every good little American, Japanese or Russian is meant to grow up identifying with and believing in the superiority of America, Japan, Russia or wherever. It's all rather absurd when you stop to think about it.

But for our rulers it's also very necessary. They want it to be so all-pervasive, so obvious, that we never stop to think about it. Patriotism reinforces the idea that there is an overriding common interest uniting boss and worker, exploiter and exploited, in this little patch of the world against bosses and workers elsewhere. And secondly it strengthens the power and authority of the state, which is the main force maintaining the rule of the exploiter over the exploited. That's why Marxists are not nationalists, but internationalists. We see the world in class terms, not national terms.

This issue marks one of the clear dividing lines between reformists and revolutionaries, between those who accept the framework of the nation state and those who want to overthrow it. Listen to any speech by any reformist politician, left or right. You will find it full of phrases such as 'saving our industry' or 'getting our country going again'. But it's not 'our' industry or 'our' country:

both are owned lock, stock and barrel by the ruling class. Every time the reformists talk this way they show themselves to be prisoners of ruling-class ideology. At the same time they strengthen such ideas within the working class.

Just as the bourgeoisie needs nationalism to bind the working class to itself, so the working class needs internationalism to establish its political independence as a class. Internationalism is also a necessity for the working class because, as the example of Russia shows, the revolution can succeed in one country for a time but if it remains isolated it cannot survive indefinitely. Either international capitalism will overthrow it directly or, as in Russia, military and economic pressure will compel the revolutionary country to compete with capitalism on the latter's terms. That means the restoration of exploitation, class divisions and the subordination of labour to capital.

Internationalism is increasingly a necessity even in everyday trade union struggles. Faced with multinational companies playing off workers in different countries against each other, the best defence is international links between rank-and-file trade unionists. 'Workers of the World Unite' isn't just a fine sounding phrase.

Marxist internationalism means rejecting the policy of import controls. Apart from the fact that they would be an economic disaster because of retaliation from other countries, they replace a struggle to defend jobs against the attacks of the British ruling class with an attempt to solve unemployment by lining up with 'our' bosses against the workers of Japan, Hong Kong, Germany, France or wherever.

Genuine internationalism involves much more than abandoning the cruder forms of national and racial prejudice and adopting a benevolent attitude to the peoples of the world. Nor is it a matter of an idealistic belief in 'the brotherhood of man' (or 'the sisterhood of women'). Indeed it is a fundamental element of Marxist internationalism that not all men are brothers and not all women are sisters because society is divided into classes with antagonistic interests.

Instead of viewing the world from the standpoint of one national state competing with other nation states, Marxist internationalism takes as its starting point the struggle of the world working class against world capitalism. In this struggle we regard the interests of the class as a whole, internationally, as taking precedence over the temporary, short-term interests of any local or national section of the class. This kind of internationalism constitutes a very sharp break with policies declared to be 'in the national interest' by the media and labour movement leaders alike.

What about immigration?

The leaders of all the main political parties are agreed that there needs to be strict control of immigration. So, probably, are most 'members of the general public'. Marxists, however, are opposed to all immigration controls. Why?

The first and most important reason is that immigration controls are racist. For a long time now 'immigrant' has served as a code word for 'black' (despite the fact that the majority of immigrants coming into Britain each year are not black, but from Europe, Australia and the USA). All the various laws introduced to limit immigration, from the original Commonwealth Immigration Act of 1962 to the Tory Nationality Act of 1980, have had as their main purpose stopping black people coming to Britain. Whenever a politician starts talking about 'the immigration problem' you can be sure that they are trying to mobilise, and cash in on, the racism that is so deeply rooted in British capitalist society.

The argument that always comes up in this context (usually from 'moderates') is that immigration must be controlled to ensure good 'race relations'. This is both hypocritical and covertly racist. It involves saying to people 'we don't want you to be racist because it's not very nice and causes a lot of trouble', and at the same time saying 'but we recognise that black people *are* a problem and we'll do our best to keep them out'. Immigration controls increase rather than hinder the growth of racism. They concede to the outright racists of the National Front and the Tory Monday Club the main point, namely that black people are a problem.

Marxists, of course, make no concessions at all to this rubbish. It is not blacks but *racism* that is the problem, the legacy of Britain's long history of imperialism (and, before that, the slave trade). It remains a powerful mechanism for dividing the working class and for diverting its anger on to vulnerable scapegoats. We must fight it tooth and nail.

This alone is more than sufficient grounds to oppose immigration controls. But even if there was no element of racism involved, if for example all the potential immigrants were white, Marxists would still be against immigration controls. It has been a consistent theme of ruling-class propaganda that social problems such as poverty, unemployment and the housing shortage are caused by there being *too many people*. This is a convenient excuse for the system. Every additional person entering the country is simultaneously an extra mouth to feed, person to be housed etc. *and* an extra worker to produce the food, build the houses and so on. If capitalism doesn't employ them do do this necessary work it is not because there are too many people, but because the capitalist economy is in crisis and because it is concerned with profit, not human need.

When capitalism is in boom and capitalists are falling over themselves to expand their operations there is usually a labour shortage. This is overcome by drawing people into the labour force from wherever there is a cheap and convenient supply: women from the home, peasants from the countryside, immigrants from poorer countries. When the boom turns to slump nothing suits the system better than to be able to treat these workers as 'surplus to requirements' and to suggest they are responsible for the crisis.

Marxists reject this logic. We approach this question, as all others, not from the standpoint of a particular capitalist state, but from the standpoint of the interests of the international working class. These are best served by the free movement of workers around the globe. Not only does this enable workers as a whole to get the best price for the sale of their labour power, it also increases the international experience of the class and aids its ultimate international unification. We therefore reject completely all attempts by the ruling class to restrict or control the international migration of labour.

So do socialists oppose national liberation movements?

The fact that Marxists are internationalists who work for the world-wide unity of the working class does not mean we are indifferent to *national* oppression. On the contrary we are its fiercest opponents. Marx, for example, was a lifelong supporter of independence for Poland, which then, as now, was oppressed by Russia, and independence for Ireland, then, as now, oppressed by Britain.

It may seem there is a contradiction here: *internationalists* supporting *national* liberation. However the real question is how international unity is to be achieved.

Firstly Marxists are for voluntary, not forced, international unity, and voluntary unity implies the right of separation. National oppression creates a *division* between the working class of the oppressor nation and the working class of the oppressed nation. This division can only be healed if the working class in the oppressor nation fights for the self-determination of the oppressed nation.

At the same time national oppression creates a certain ideological *bond* between the ruling class and the working class in both the oppressor nation and the oppressed. Both these bonds can only be broken if the working class opposes national oppression, especially when perpetrated by its own state. Opposition to all national oppression is therefore an essential part of real internationalism.

The rise of imperialism made this question central to socialist strategy. By the end of the 19th century a handful of advanced capitalist countries had turned most of Africa, Asia and Latin America into their colonies or semi-colonies. At the time much of the European socialist movement either openly supported or, at best, passively accepted this development. It was Lenin who saw that imperialism would inevitably generate struggles for national liberation and who argued that the working class of the advanced countries must establish an alliance with the national liberation movements against the imperialist ruling classes.

Today the nature of imperialism has somewhat changed and in most cases these colonies have been granted formal independence while the pressure of the world market ensures that their economic exploitation continues. But national liberation struggles are by no means a thing of the past. In El Salvador and Nicaragua, in Poland and Eritrea, in Ireland, in Israel and the Lebanon the fight against national oppression continues, whether that oppression is perpetrated by the United States, or Stalinist Russia, or Zionism. In all these cases Marxists give their unconditional support to the freedom fighters.

However, unconditional is not the same as uncritical. Nor does support for national liberation mean overestimating its significance. The achievement of national independence is a bourgeois democratic not a socialist task, and national revolution is not a socialist revolution unless it is led by the working class. Even then it can't be sustained unless it becomes part of a process of international revolution.

This is particularly important because the period since 1945 has seen a succession of national revolutions led by bourgeois or petty bourgeois forces calling themselves communist or socialist. China, Cuba, Vietnam, Angola, Mozambique, Zimbabwe are some of the main examples.

In none of these cases has the working class actually come to power, yet many on the left have sought to substitute these anti-imperialist movements for the struggle of the working class in both the advanced countries and in the third world itself. Their attitude has led to repeated disillusionment as each of these regimes has failed in its apparent promise.

Marxists therefore oppose all forms of national oppression and support the struggle for national liberation, but do so as internationalists not nationalists. We do not merge with bourgeois nationalism or drop our criticism of its limitations. Instead we work to bring to the fore the working class both as the leader of the national revolution and at the same time as a part of the international working class — the only force that can bring real liberation from capitalism and imperialism and unite the human race.

What do you mean by 'unconditional but critical' support?

Let's take a current and important example. What should the attitude of Marxists be to the African National Congress, one of the leading forces in the black struggle against apartheid?

The answer is clear. First of all we support the ANC *unreservedly and unconditionally* against the racist South African regime. We defend its right to take up arms against the repressive state; we call for the release of its political prisoners and we applaud its courage and its victories.

At the same time we are critical of the ANC's political line and practice. We criticise its belief in a cross-class alliance of all blacks and 'progressive' whites, and its relative neglect of the role of the black industrial working class. We also disagree with its 'stages' theory, by which it separates the struggle against apartheid — the struggle for democratic political rights — from the struggle for socialism itself. For this leads to a willingness to negotiate and compromise with the representatives of white capital. Experience in other parts of the world has shown that this gives political rights to the middle class while leaving workers little better off.

However, our attitude to the ANC is only one example of a general stance — unconditional but critical support — which Marxists take towards numerous movements round the world today. For example we support the Sandinistas in Nicaragua against US intervention and the Contras but criticise their alliance with the Nicaraguan bourgeoisie and their maintenance of capitalism. Another example is the IRA, who we support against British imperialism and the Orange reactionaries but criticise for their reliance on terrorism and failure to mobilise the working class.

This is a position which people often find difficult to grasp. It seems to them a contradiction. Surely, they think, if you support a movement you shouldn't criticise it. Or, conversely, if you criticise it you can't really support it. Consequently, the position of critical support comes under fire from a number of directions.

From the right it is argued that if a movement pursues tactics or undertakes actions (say planting bombs) which we regard as wrong then that movement should be condemned. From the ultra-left it is sometimes argued that since Marxists have important differences with national liberation movements we should give them no support whatever. From other sections of the left (particularly the romantic left) comes the emotive argument that since these movements and their leaders display immense courage we have therefore no right to criticise them at all.

All these arguments are wrong.

The right-wing argument is wrong because movements and struggles should be judged primarily not by particular actions and tactics but by the social forces they represent. To condemn a movement of the oppressed on the grounds of its tactics, even where those tactics are clearly mistaken (as with the IRA Birmingham pub bombing in 1974), is to give tacit or open support to the oppressor.

The ultra-left argument is wrong because, albeit from different motives, in refusing to support national liberation struggles it arrives at the same objective position as the right wing, and is therefore self-defeating. There is no neutrality in the class struggle. Marxists are part of the working class, part of the oppressed and part of the left. Its victories are our victories, its defeats our defeats, no matter who the leaders or what the tactics may be.

The argument for supporting liberation movements without criticism is also wrong. Courage and heroism should always be given their due but they are no guarantee of tactics that can win or of a political line that represents the interests of the working class. The IRA fights bravely, but its military strategy cannot defeat the British army; the Iranian masses braved the hideous repression of the Shah only to install the Ayatollah Khomeini's Islamic republic. To abandon criticism is to abandon Marxist principles and therefore to abandon our defence of the interests of the working class.

'Unconditional but critical support' is thus an essential position for Marxists. It is crucial for all our political work not only in relation to national liberation movements but also in the British class struggle. We supported wholeheartedly the struggle of the Liverpool Labour councillors against the Tory government, but we criticise their inadequate strategy. If tomorrow the general secretary of the TGWU finds himself before the courts for breaking Tory anti-union laws we will mobilise in his support, but we won't drop our criticisms of him as a trade union bureaucrat.

Without the combination of *both* support and criticism, Marxists are condemned to either sterile sectarianism or crude opportunism.

What happened in Russia?

The Russian Revolution of 1917 proved that revolution can succeed, that the working class can overthrow capitalism, and take control of society — but it also confirmed the Marxist view that a socialist revolution could survive only if it were part of an international revolution. On this Marx, Engels, Lenin, Trotsky — indeed all Marxists before Stalin — had insisted.

Russia today is a result, not of the revolution of 1917, but of the *defeat* of that revolution by the Stalinist counter-revolution of the 1920s. How this defeat came about is extremely important for all socialists to understand. The essence of the 1917 revolution was the establishment of workers' power through the rule of Soviets or workers' councils. Both the revolution and the functioning of the Soviets depended on a working class with a high level of political consciousness, activity and enthusiasm. In 1917 the Russian working class possessed these qualities in abundance, but in the years following the revolution it lost them.

This was not because of some 'natural law' that revolution must fail, but because of the material conditions prevailing in Russia at the time. Above all it was because of the hideous civil war of 1918-21, backed by Britain, France and other imperialist powers. The civil war claimed the lives of a huge proportion of the most politically advanced workers who formed the core of the revolutionary Red Army. It also utterly devastated the Russian economy. Industry and transport ground to a halt. Factories stood idle, famine and epidemics raged. Many workers fled to the countryside in search of food. By 1921 the total number of industrial workers had fallen from three million to one and a quarter million, and those that remained were politically exhausted. They were simply unable to maintain the control over society they had won in October 1917.

In the absence of an active working class the Bolsheviks were forced to rely more and more on the old Tsarist officials to administer the country. In the process they themselves tended to become a bureaucracy divorced from popular control. The individual who personified and led this development was Joseph Stalin.

The rise of Stalinism did not go unresisted. Lenin himself devoted the last months of his life, when he was incapacitated by illness, to a desperate struggle against bureaucracy in general and Stalin in particular. Subsequently almost all the leading Bolsheviks made some attempt to block the path of the Stalinist counter-revolution, and Trotsky remained its uncompromising opponent until his death. But all the social conditions favoured the bureaucracy, and step by step Stalin and his supporters were able to defeat their opponents until by the end of the 1920s, all effective opposition was eliminated and all workers' rights were removed.

The only thing that could have prevented the rise of the bureaucracy was international revolution. If the revolution had spread rapidly to other European countries (as it nearly did in 1918-19) the civil war would have been won before the working class was decimated. Even as late as 1923, revolution in Germany (a real possibility) would have transformed the situation. It would have brought aid to poverty-stricken Russia and so strengthened the workers. It would have removed the threat of intervention and with it the need to compete militarily and economically with Western capitalism.

After 1923 the bureaucracy turned its back on the international revolution. It was concerned with developing its own power, not spreading workers' power. Hence Stalin's policy of 'socialism in one country'. In practice this meant strengthening the Russian state in competition with the West, by exploiting the workers and peasants. The system was, and is, *state capitalism*.

From Stalin to Gorbachev the basic structure of power has remained unchanged. Russia today is nothing to do with socialism.

It is the opposite of socialism. But the real lesson of the Russian Revolution is not that socialist revolution can't work. It is that revolution must spread internationally.

Was China any different?

China, with its billion-strong population and its vast land area, was in 1949 the scene of the twentieth century's second great revolution. Yet nowadays China is hardly mentioned on the left.

It wasn't always so. In the sixties China was a major influence on what was then known as the New Left. Generally speaking China was seen as offering an attractive alternative model of socialist construction far more dynamic and revolutionary than Russia.

The decade of the 1970s was ruthless with these hopes and illusions. It saw China enter into open alliance with US imperialism, make war on Vietnam, support the murderous Pol Pot regime in Kampuchea and the South African-backed 'Unita' in Angola, and generally pursue a foreign policy worthy of Franco's Spain. Internally it saw the public renunciation of the cultural revolution and much of the legacy of Mao, the opening of China to foreign capital, and even flirtation with such evidently bourgeois values as fashion and consumerism.

Small wonder then that Chinese sympathisers were disillusioned. China became a bad dream best forgotten. But the current silence about China on the left represents more than just disappointment. It also marks a failure of understanding and analysis. For events in China could be understood (and indeed predicted) only with the aid of the Marxist theory of state capitalism, first developed in relation to Russia.

The Chinese Revolution of 1949, for all its scale and grandeur, was never a workers' revolution. The working class played no active role in it whatsoever. Rather it was a military victory in which a peasant-based army led by a middle-class political elite conquered the cities from the outside. The result was not workers' control or workers' power, still less socialism, but the establishment of the political elite as a new ruling class. The aim of this new ruling class, despite its radical rhetoric, was not world revolution but the independent, national development of China in competition with the rest of world capitalism.

The very low level of economic development in China necessitated the extraction of a high level of exploitation of its workers and peasants. The numerous power struggles within Chinese Communism were about how to achieve the aim of national development, not about the goal itself — which was shared by all factions.

Once this basic dynamic of the regime is understood, recent events in China are cause for neither surprise nor despondency. China broke from Russia in the late 1950s because it did not wish to become a Russian client state like Poland or Hungary. For a while it attempted to develop its economy alone in opposition to both the superpowers. The failure of this attempt has forced it to establish links with more developed economies.

The importance of all this for Marxists is that it was the decisive test for the kind of third world nationalist 'socialism' many on the left still worship from afar. In terms of traditions and language Mao stood far closer to Marxism than Castro or the Sandinistas. In terms of size and resources it was far better placed than Nicaragua or Tanzania to achieve independent economic development. But China has neither achieved socialism nor even sustained its economic independence from international capital.

The fate of the Chinese Revolution provides crucial confirmation of two basic Marxist propositions: firstly that there is no substitute for the working class as the agent of socialism, and secondly that capitalism has created an integrated world economy from which there is no ultimate escape except through world revolution.

But isn't a simultaneous world revolution impossible?

Yes, a world revolution that takes place everywhere at once is impossible or extremely unlikely. But this isn't what Marxists are talking about. What we are proposing is that successfully carrying out a revolution in one country can become the *starting* point for spreading the revolution internationally. This was the strategy proposed by Lenin and Trotsky, and it is one that is entirely realistic.

Socialism in one country is impossible because sooner or later world capitalism will either overthrow an isolated revolution by military force or it will do what it did to Russia. The isolated Russian economy was forced to compete in a world market on terms laid down by capitalism. The result was the restoration of capitalist economic relations. Russian workers suffered super-exploitation as Stalin built new industries to compete with the West.

But the return of exploitation was not inevitable. There was an alternative road, presented by Leon Trotsky, who began from the perspective of spreading the revolution. There are a number of reasons why this was possible — and why it would be possible in any truly revolutionary upheaval.

Firstly, the crisis of capitalism which creates the conditions for revolutionary upheavals would be an international not a national crisis. This is bound to be the case because the capitalist economy is fully international: every national economy is integrated into that world economy. As a result the conditions creating the revolution in one country would exist in many other countries at the same time.

Secondly, the victory of the working class in one country would inspire workers in other countries to follow their example. It would show workers could take power and raise workers' confidence enormously. An outline would exist of the basic strategy and tactics to be used.

Thirdly, the existence of workers' power in one country would provide a focus from which a worldwide revolutionary movement could be supported and organised. This doesn't mean imposing revolution by force. It means drawing together the most advanced workers of all countries to discuss how the fight for workers' power could be carried on and how the maximum international solidarity for the revolutionary struggle could be mobilised.

All these factors were at work in the years following the Russian Revolution. The First World War, which helped cause the revolution, also plunged all of Europe into a revolutionary storm. The German Emperor was overthrown and the Austrian Empire collapsed. In Bavaria and Hungary there were shortlived Soviet Republics. In Germany the revolution seemed set to succeed in both 1919 and 1923 while Italy saw a massive wave of factory occupations in 1920.

The Russian Revolution was a tremendous encouragement to those workers involved. The idea of soviets — or workers' councils — as the basis for workers' power, was taken up by the workers of many countries during the course of the struggle. And in 1919 the Bolsheviks were able to found the Communist International — organising revolutionary workers worldwide.

But the revolutionary wave was defeated — and capitalism survived — though it waas a close thing. Today the possibility of such an international wave of revolution is even greater than in 1917 to 1923. The development of capitalism has strengthened its international nature. The working class in every country is larger and has greater economic power than in Russia in 1917. The development of international communications and transport has made international contact far easier . Such developments will increase the impact of any revolutionary breakthrough and help spread the ideas of workers' power.

Chapter Seven:
Strategies for socialism

'But we've already got a mass workers' party . . .'

'THE LABOUR PARTY is the mass party of the working class.' This familiar claim is usually made as part of an argument that Marxists should abandon the attempt to build an independent revolutionary party and join the Labour Party.

At first sight it is a claim that seems to have a lot of truth in it. Certainly no other party is in a position to make such a claim and certainly a large proportion of the working class (frequently a majority) have regularly voted for it since 1945. It is also the case that the Labour Party was set up by, and has always retained a close relationship with, the trade unions — which undoubtedly are mass working-class organisations.

These are important facts which should not be lost sight of. They clearly distinguish the Labour Party not only from the Conservative Party — a direct representative of the ruling class — but also from the Social Democrats and the Liberals, neither of which have such an organisational connection with the working class. Because of this, when it comes to a choice between Labour and any of these other parties, as at a general election, Marxists will not abstain, but will support Labour.

Nevertheless these facts alone do not not at all suffice as the basis for a Marxist analysis of the class character of the Labour Party. It is necessary also to consider the nature of the party's programme, its leadership, and above all its actual practice, in order to make an overall assessment of its role in the class struggle.

First the programme. The Labour Party does not have a specific document which constitutes its official programme. Its constitution, of course, contains the famous Clause Four commitment to the 'common ownership of the means of production, distribution and exchange', but this has never been taken seriously, even for inclusion in election manifestos. In general terms, however, and this applies to both its manifestos and the beliefs of the vast majority of its members at all levels, Labour's programme is the reform of capitalism through parliament. For the right wing, the centre and even the 'soft left' of the party, this means a quite definite acceptance of the need to keep capitalism going while carrying through reforms.

Only sections of the 'hard left' even contemplate the idea of actually trying to abolish capitalism by means of systematic reforms, and they are ever willing to collaborate with and capitulate to the centre and the right.

The leadership of the party has lain always with the centre and right. When it has appeared to be captured by the left this has invariably proved illusory as the 'left' has moved rapidly rightwards. In terms of their social position, Labour's leading figures have been at the very least upper middle class and in many cases closely integrated into the ruling class itself. The other dominant force in the party are the top trade union bureaucrats who supply the bulk of the funds and control the annual conference through the block vote system. They form a distinct and privileged layer standing above the working class.

The practice of the Labour Party needs to be considered in terms of its relationship to actual workers' struggles in industry and in the workplace, and in terms of its behaviour in government. Where the former is concerned, its role is minimal. Most strikes it simply ignores, leaving them to the unions, and when a struggle is so important that it has to take some notice it either 'supports' from the sidelines, or equivocates, or tries to play a mediating role in order to get a settlement. In no way does the Labour Party attempt to offer organised political leadership to the industrial struggle.

In government the Labour Party has repeatedly shown its

preference for the priorities and requirements of capitalism over the needs of the working people it claims it represents. Again and again it has attacked strikes, raised unemployment, held down wages through incomes policies and cut spending on health and education.

Thus in neither programme, nor leadership, nor practice is the Labour Party the 'party of the working class'. Rather it is a *capitalist* party operating within the working-class movement. Its role in the class struggle is to give just enough expression to working-class discontent to contain this discontent within the structures of capitalism. It is, together with the trade union bureaucracy, a principal prop and defender of the capitalist order.

One further element of the original claim needs to be challenged, namely the idea that Labour is a *mass* party. In electoral terms it is, and also in its affiliated trade union membership, but this support is overwhelmingly passive. Its individual, real, membership is not above 300,000 and of these not more than about one in ten are active. The party cannot even sustain its own mass circulation newspaper.

The conclusion is inescapable. The 'mass party of the British working class' does not yet exist.

Can the Labour Party be changed?

Could Labour be changed into a socialist party that really represents and fights for the interests of working-class people? History suggests otherwise.

For 80 years the Labour Party has been sustained by people on the left who were trying to change it. Overwhelmingly the experience has been not of them changing the Labour Party but of the Labour Party changing them.

Leader after leader, Ramsey MacDonald, Attlee, Wilson, Foot, Kinnock, have begun on the left and then progressed to the right, and they are only the tip of the iceberg. Beneath them are innumerable lesser figures who have been subject to the same process of gradual political corruption — 'radical firebrands' turned into 'respectable moderates' if not worse. Manny Shinwell, Stafford

Cripps, John Strachey and Barbara Castle are fine examples from the past. Tariq Ali, Peter Hain, Ted Knight and Ken Livingstone are currently undergoing the treatment.

Even determined Marxists with revolutionary origins (such as the Militant Tendency) are not immune to the process. Years and years of trying to change the Labour Party and they become acclimatised to its reformist routine, embroiled in its structures and end up compromising their politics on the tough (but crucial) issues such as the Falklands War and Northern Ireland or on the question of a parliamentary road to socialism.

However, it is not just past experience that testifies against the possibility of changing the Labour Party, it is also any realistic assessment of the nature of the Labour Party today. First there is the fact that there is still very little that the party rank and file can do to control the behaviour of Labour MPs and *nothing* it can do to control the actions of a Labour government. Consequently any amount of left-wing resolutions on nationalising the commanding heights of the economy or unilateral disarmament can be won at Labour conferences without the least guarantee that anything will be done about them.

Secondly there is the role of the trade union leaders. Their position in the Labour Party is crucial because they supply the bulk of party funds and they dominate the conference and all the elections through the block vote system. The power of these trade union bosses will always be used against any real socialist transformation of the Labour Party, because the trade union bureaucracy is itself undemocratic and privileged in relation to the trade union rank and file. Thus in order to thoroughly democratise and radicalise the Labour Party it would first be necessary to thoroughly democratise and radicalise the trade unions.

Thirdly the whole structure and organisation of the Labour Party reflects the fact that it is essentially an electoral machine, designed to elect Labour MPs rather than advance the interests of the working class in struggle. The basic units of the party are wards and constituency parties, not workplace branches. The bulk of the membership are passive card-holders except at election times. The transformation of the Labour Party into a fighting socialist party would involve reshaping it and rebuilding it from top to bottom.

The only circumstances in which such a total overhaul of the Labour Party might even be seriously attempted is in the context of *mass* radicalisation of the working class, which in turn can occur only in the midst of mass revolutionary struggles.

The mass of workers will come to socialism not through reading papers and listening to speeches but through their experience of great class-wide battles. Such revolutionary situations in which the majority of the working class become activated do not, by their nature, last long (perhaps eighteen months at most). At any rate not long enough for the laborious process of purging and remaking the Labour Party. Consequently unless at least the foundations of a revolutionary workers' party have been laid in advance of these decisive battles, the right wing and reformist leadership will still be able to use that power and influence to secure the defeat of the working class and the return to capitalist 'normality'.

One argument remains — the negative one that not to be in the Labour Party is to be isolated from the labour movement. But this is to confuse the Labour Party and the labour movement. The basic organisations of the working class are not the Labour Party but the trade unions. So long as socialists make it a point of principle to be active in their workplaces and their unions they can both be part of the labour movement *and* build an independent revolutionary party. In the long run this is a far more realistic project than pursuing the pipedream of changing the Labour Party!

Couldn't we do without organisation?

Marxism has always had to compete with rival theories. Its main rivals, apart from straightforward capitalist ideology, have been social democratic reformism and Stalinism. But there has usually been another alternative standing, apparently, to the left of Marxism, namely anarchism.

Anarchism clearly is not an important political force in Britain today, but at various times in the history of the revolutionary movement (most notably in the Spanish Civil War) it has exercised some considerable influence. Even now it has definite attractions for the young and rebellious.

First let us be clear that Marxists cannot afford simply to scorn anarchism in the way capitalist 'common sense' does. This is because the ultimate goal of anarchism — a society of real freedom and equality in which there is no longer a state or any form of oppression of people by people — is one that Marxists share. Supporters of the present order dismiss such an aim as absurd. Marxists do not. Our disagreements with anarchism are not over the ultimate aim but over how to achieve it; that is, how society is to be changed.

The starting point of this disagreement is a different view of the root cause of exploitation and oppression. To the anarchist the root cause is power: power in and of itself, power in all its forms — state power, the power of political parties and unions and every other kind of authority and leadership.

Anarchists believe that it is the existence of this power and authority which *creates* class divisions and all other kinds of inequality and oppression. Their 'strategy' therefore is to denounce and renounce, on principle, all manifestations of power and authority, and above all every kind of state power. To these they counterpose the absolute freedom of the individual and the purely spontaneous rebellion of the masses.

Anarchism is thus essentially a moral stance. It lacks any historical analysis of how the things it opposes came about or of why it should be possible to get rid of them now, rather than any time in the past. It simply condemns 'evil' and fights for 'good'.

In contrast Marxism does not regard the state (or 'power' in general) as the *fundamental* problem. Rather it explains the emergence of the state as the product of the division of society into antagonistic classes. This in turn is explained as the consequence of a certain stage in the development of the forces of production. The central task therefore is the abolition of class divisions. This can be achieved only through the victory of the working class over the capitalist class. For this the working class requires organisation and leadership (trade unions, the revolutionary party, workers' councils, and so on), and the use of power — from the mass picket up to and including the creation of its own workers' state to combat counter-revolution.

It is this last point which arouses the particular ire of the anarchist. Here they echo the bourgeois arguments: that revolutionary power leads inevitably to tyranny; that Leninism leads inevitably to Stalinism. However, anarchism has failed to come up with any serious alternative way of dealing with the resistance of the capitalists and their efforts to restore the old order.

So far we have been discussing 'pure' anarchism which has its social base in the radical petty bourgeoisie — which feels alienated from both the power of big capital and the power of the working class. In so far as anarchism has attempted to gain a base in the working class, it has had to abandon some of its individualist principles and accept the need for collective organisation. Thus it has tended to merge with *syndicalism*, a form of revolutionary trade unionism which rejects participation in 'bourgeois' politics and the role of the revolutionary party.

It is as anarcho-syndicalism that anarchism has come closest to Marxism, and in the wake of the Russian Revolution many anarcho-syndicalists were drawn to the Communist International. But anarchism's lack of theory, its abstention from politics, leaves the field to the reformists. Its failure to think through the realities of workers' power disqualify anarchism as a practical guide to the achievement of the revolutionary transformation of society and the emancipation of the working class.

So trade unions have a role to play?

The relationship between the trade union struggle and the struggle for socialism is not a new question. It has been around since the beginnings of trade union and socialist movements in the early part of the nineteenth century. It is therefore useful to look back to what Marx himself said about it, especially as it was one of the great weaknesses of the socialists before Marx that they tended to ignore the trade unions.

'When it is a question', wrote Marx in 1846, 'of making a precise study of strikes, unions and other forms in which workers carry out before our eyes their organisation as a class, some are seized with real fear and others display a transcendantal disdain.'

The reason for this 'fear' and 'disdain' was that most early socialists came from the middle class and looked to this class to achieve socialism, either through moral persuasion of the ruling class or through secret conspiracies on the model of the French Revolution of 1789. Marx, however, rejected both moral persuasion and secret conspiracies in favour of class struggle by the workers themselves. Consequently he immediately recognised the crucial importance of trade unions and strikes as the basic way in which workers organised to defend themselves against the employers and built their unity for the future overthrow of capitalism.

But Marx also pointed out the limitations of the trade union struggle. The starting point of trade unionism was the attempt to improve the terms on which workers sold their labour power to the bosses, not to overthrow the boss-worker relationship altogether.

What was needed therefore was not only trade union organisation but also political organisation: the creation of a workers' political party which would continually raise within the broader workers' movement the key questions of political power and the ownership of the means of production.

Since Marx's day these debates have continued. During the early years of the 20th century the workers' movement internationally was divided into Social Democrats (like the British Labour Party) and syndicalists (like the American Wobblies). The Social Democrats looked to parliament (a later version of moral persuasion) to achieve socialism, and recognised strike action only for limited economic purposes. The syndicalists, reacting against the parliamentarianism of the Social Democrats, rejected the whole idea of political parties in favour of militant trade unionism.

Both strategies proved inadequate, particularly in the sharpened conditions of the First World War, and it was left to Lenin and the Bolsheviks to develop the Marxist position of building a revolutionary political party within all the daily struggles of the working class.

These different approaches reappeared in relation to the British miners' strike of 1984-5. Labour Party leaders, despite depending on the unions for votes and money, regard political struggle as something to wage through parliament. They therefore reacted to the strike with embarassment in case it cost them votes. Various middle-class socialists also turned up their noses at the trade union struggle because it was 'only' about economic issues. But there were hundreds of thousands of workers who supported the strike and even saw that it could politically weaken the Tories — but did not see it as part of an overall struggle against capitalism.

The Marxist tradition is closest to the last of these in that we were 100 per cent in support of the strike and would do everything we could to help it win. But we also recognised that, while a victory for the miners would also strengthen the struggle for socialism as a whole by defeating the Tories, hoever great this victory, trade union action alone would not be enough. So within the strike and in the course of solidarity work around it we were simultaneously working to draw workers to revolutionary socialist ideas and to the building of a revolutionary party.

What about nationalisation?

One of the most widespread myths about Marxism is that it is first and foremost a doctrine of nationalisation and state ownership. This is a myth that is constantly and deliberately encouraged by the ruling class in order to discredit Marxism. Knowing that people generally resent and fear the state bureaucracy, the ruling class puts it about that Marxists want to expand the power of this bureaucracy till it controls everything — like in Eastern Europe.

Unfortunately it is a myth that is also believed and encouraged by many who call themselves Marxists. This is particularly the case with those who call countries like Russia and Poland 'socialist' simply on the grounds that their economies are nationalised — despite the fact that they have not a shred of workers' democracy. It also applies to those who talk of a Labour government introducing socialism by nationalising the 'commanding heights' of the economy, or the 'top 200 monopolies' as they sometimes put it.

In fact the central idea of Marxism is not nationalisation but class struggle — the struggle of the working class for self-emancipation — leading to the abolition of class divisions and the withering away of the state. Of course Marxists support nationalisation, but as a *means* through which the working class can take collective control, not as an end in itself. Our aim, therefore, is nationalisation not by the existing capitalist state but by a workers' state and with full workers' control.

Without workers' power and workers' control nationalisation is not socialism but state capitalism — a further extension of the concentration of capital into larger and larger units. As Engels put it, 'The more the state proceeds to the taking over of productive forces the more does it actually become the national capitalist . . . The capitalist relation is not done away with. It is rather brought to a head.'

Clear proof of this is the behaviour of British Steel, British Rail and the National Coal Board. Far from being islands of socialism in the capitalist sea, they ruthlessly exploit their workforce for the sake of profit just like other capitalist industries. Indeed, in recent years they have been at the centre of the ruling-class assault on jobs, wages and union organisation.

Some people suggest this is because the nationalised industries are only a minority of British industry, most of which remains in private hands. But in Russia, where the state owns almost all the means of production, workers are still exploited and oppressed, and production still serves the accumulation of capital rather than human needs. *It is only in conjunction with workers' power that nationalisation signifies a break with capitalism.*

Does it follow from this that Marxists should be indifferent to the current Tory drive towards 'privatisation'? Not at all. In the first place privatisation goes hand-in-hand with an attack on jobs and working conditions and must be resisted as such. In the second place it generally involves an attack on the quality of service provided by the industry concerned, which must also be resisted.

Institutions like the National Health Service and state education make a real difference to the standard of living of working people. Their defence is a matter of central concern to Marxists. Equally the demand for nationalisation of a company that goes bankrupt can be an important weapon in the struggle to save the jobs of the workforce. (Certainly it's far better than setting up a workers' co-op.)

However, in all these cases what we are talking about is reforms *within* capitalism, not measures that overthrow it, or even initiate its overthrow. Marxists are the most determined fighters for reforms because it is through fighting for reforms that workers build their consciousness, confidence and fighting spirit. But that is no reason to confuse these reforms with socialism, the basis of which is, and can only be, the establishment of workers' power.

What we mean by revolutionary leadership

The standard right-wing view of revolution sees it as a conspiracy engineered by malicious revolutionaries with the mass of people playing only the role of passive bystanders. Clearly this is a stupid caricature. But sometimes, especially when the majority of workes *are* passive, would-be revolutionaries and others on the left can adopt a kind of mirror image of this reactionary view. They see revolutionaries as heroic individuals acting *on behalf of* the working class to liberate them from above.

Carried to its extreme, this sort of thinking leads to terrorism and the kind of actions undertaken by the Italian Red Brigades. It has a long history stretching back to the nineteenth century French revolutionary Blanqui, who devoted his life to planning insurrections to be carried through by a special selected elite.

The Marxist view is very different. As Trotsky put it, 'the most indubitable feature of a revolution is the direct interference of the masses in historic events . . . a revolution is first of all the forcible entrance of the masses into the realm of rulership over their own destiny.'

This principle is confirmed by all the experience of workers' revolutions in the past century and a half. From the Paris Commune of 1871 to the Russian Revolution of 1917, and more recently the May events in France 1968 and the Solidarity movement in Poland, every major confrontation between workers and the existing order has begun spontaneously — not at the summons or behest of a revolutionary organisation.

This in no way invalidates the role of revolutionary leadership. Revolutions may begin spontaneously but they do not end that way. Either in the course of the revolutionary upheaval a revolutionary party is able to win the leadership of the masses, then organise and centralise them for the seizure of power (as was the case in Russia) or the revolution will eventually be stifled and defeated. Nevertheless, the role of the party is to guide the revolution to victory, not to manufacture it. The role of revolutionaries is to lead the masses, not to substitute for them.

All of this may seem obvious in the abstract when we are talking about a full-scale revolution — no one is going to argue that the Socialist Workers Party can overthrow the Tory government by mounting a surprise attack on Downing Street. But it also applies to the thousands of partial economic and political struggles that occur in non-revolutionary and pre-revolutionary situations.

Here the principle can be harder to grasp. Take the case of a small local strike which socialists in the area have been actively supporting, visiting the picket line, collecting money and so on. After a few weeks the strike runs into difficulties and the picket line dwindles. Here there can be a strong temptation for socialist supporters to substitute themselves for the workers on the picket line rather than arguing for a strategy that can reinvolve them.

Another example is Ireland. British rule in Northern Ireland has been and remains brutal and oppressive and socialists have a duty to say so loud and clear. But the fact is that for the last ten years there has been no mass campaign in Britain on the Irish question. Some very small revolutionary groups see this as the fault of somewhat larger revolutionary groups. In reality, neither the SWP nor any other left organisation could create such a campaign by sheer willpower in the total absence of a mood of solidarity in at least a section of the working class (above all Irish workers in Britain).

Finally there is the case of a battle such as that of the printers at 'Fortress Wapping', where workers fought for their jobs against pre-planned mass strike-breaking, organised by the employer and heavily defended by the forces of the state — the police. From the outset it was obvious to revolutionary socialists that the first step towards winning this vital dispute was a series of militant mass pickets. At the same time it was no less obvious that the trade union leaders were not prepared to organise such pickets, indeed actively opposed them.

In such a situation the substitutionist temptation is there again. Perhaps what the printers aren't doing we should do for them? Perhaps if every **Socialist Worker** supporter could be assembled at Wapping every Saturday night that would do the trick? Actually this is neither practical nor desirable, as it would not solve the basic problem in the dispute. The task would remain of mobilising the mass of print workers — and not just those directly involved — and then other trade unionists in their support.

Does this mean revolutionary socialists do nothing? No, it means continuing to support the pickets, and outlining to the workers involved an alternative strategy to that of the union leaders.

Revolutionary leadership is an art which involves the concrete assessment of every concrete situation — there are no universally valid rules. But in general we can say this: it is not a matter of revolutionaries leading themselves, but of drawing into action workers who are not yet revolutionaries. This means neither tail-ending the working class nor being so far ahead of it as to be out of sight.

Many campaigns — only one war

The list of injustices in our society is endless; poverty, racism, the Bomb, homelessness, cuts in health and education, the plight of old age pensioners, the treatment of the disabled, police brutality, the oppression of women and gays, repression in Ireland, attacks on the unions, unemployment. One of the crucial differences between liberals or reformists, on the one hand, and Marxists on the other, is that the former tend to regard each issue as an isolated problem capable of being solved on its own, whereas the latter view all of them as having a common root in the economic structure of capitalism.

For the liberals the way to tackle these issues is largely a matter of changing attitudes; of the enlightened — themselves — persuading the unenlightened; of influencing the powerful directly, or else of mobilising public opinion which in turn will influence the powerful.

For Marxists it is first of all a matter of mobilising the power of the oppressed themselves to win concessions from the system through struggle and, in the process, developing and harnessing that power to overthrow the system completely.

To illustrate and evaluate these different approaches, let's take two examples. First, the treatment of old age pensioners.

Everyone knows the majority of old age pensioners (those from the working class) are treated miserably. After a lifetime working for the system they are 'rewarded' with a pittance barely enough for survival. The old make up the largest single group within the 15 million people in Britain who are on the poverty line. Almost everyone would like to see pensioners treated better. Most politicians feel obliged to pay lip service to the pensioners. In an opinion poll, I would guess, 90 per cent at least would favour higher pensions. No one, as far as I know, actually opposes or attacks the pensioners. And yet, despite this immense support, their desperate situation remains unchanged. Why?

First because our society subordinates everything to the accumulation of capital, and from the point of view of capital, pensioners are useless, indeed, worse than useless. Consequently, in the queue for 'rewards' pensioners will always come light years behind the Royal Family, the armed forces, the police, Lord Mayor's banquets and innumerable other vicious or useless obscenities, all of which do contribute — in their way — to maintaining the rule of capital.

Second, because as old age pensioners they lack the collective bargaining power to force an improvement in their lot. This latter condition will remain until organised workers use their industrial strength to fight not only for themselves, but for pensioners too. The first condition will remain until production for profit is replaced by production for need.

Another example is the oppression of women. Sexist attitudes are, of course, still widespread and deeply rooted. Nonetheless in terms of 'attitudes' the past 15 years have seen an extraordinary transformation. At the level of ideas, the women's movement has been an amazing success. There have been two major pieces of legislation, the Equal Pay Act and the Sex Discrimination Act, in force for eight years. Yet the actual conditions of most women have worsened rather than improved. The earnings gap between men and women has widened and child care and housework remain overwhelmingly the responsibility of women.

Again we must ask why, and again the answer brings us back to the requirements of capitalism. For capital women remain a source of cheap labour that it will not, and cannot, afford to pass up. For capital the family structure, which oppresses women, remains an exceedingly convenient arrangement for the reproduction of labour power and maintenance of social control. Only the overthrow of capitalism will create the real conditions for women's liberation.

Both these examples point to the same conclusion. Oppression takes many forms and each form of oppression generates its own struggle for reform. Marxists support these many struggles, but they don't lose sight of the fact that the different oppressions have a common souce in the capitalist mode of production. The many struggles are not isolated campaigns, but different aspects of a single war — the war of the working class to overthrow capitalism.

Why we need a revolutionary party

Capitalism is in a state of deep economic crisis and the capitalist class always reacts to economic crisis in the same way: it attacks the working class. This has been the fundamental reality behind government policy in Britain for the last ten years or more, whether the government has been Tory or Labour. It is going to continue to be the fundamental reality facing the working class for the foreseeable future, no matter who wins the next election or the election after that.

Because the capitalist crisis is world-wide, it is true for workers everywhere. High unemployment in the USA, food queues in the Eastern bloc, starvation in the 'Third World' — all are manifestations of the way the world's ruling classes are making workers pay for the crisis.

Time and again the ruling class will return to the offensive striving to weaken union organisation, drive down wages, cut social services, slash jobs and undermine workers' rights. All with the basic aim of reducing the share of the national income going to the working class and increasing the share going to profits.

In this way they will eventually provoke a massive and general confrontation between capital and labour. We cannot tell when this will happen but we can be sure that sooner or later it will. The question facing the working class and in particular its politically aware sections, in other words socialists, is how best to prepare for this confrontation so that the working class wins it.

Marxism provides an answer to this question. It is that we should build a revolutionary party.

This is neither easy nor fashionable. It means accepting (for the present) being a small minority within the class as a whole, and it involves much hard work and numerous difficulties. Nevertheless it is essential, for the simple reason that without revolutionary leadership the working class is bound to be defeated in a decisive conflict.

The enemy we face, the ruling class, is highly organised and centralised. This applies to each company, where you can be sure that all the managers of BL, ICI and the National Coal Board will follow a single coordinated strategy, and it applies to each capitalist state, whether East or West. Obviously the army and the police are highly disciplined and act according to a centralised plan.

To defeat such an opponent the working class must also be centralised. It must be able to link its action in Glasgow, Edinburgh and Aberdeen with its action in Liverpool, Birmingham and London. It must be able to pursue the same strategy among miners, dockers, engineering workers, teachers and civil servants. Such coordination can only be supplied by an organisation which unites the workers leading the struggles in all these localities and workplaces.

At first glance the obvious candidates for this role are the trade unions and the Labour Party, with their already established mass memberships. However it is a task they are completely incapable of performing: they cannot coordinate the struggle effectively because at bottom they do not even want to wage it. Both the trade union leaders, whose main concern is to preserve their balancing role between workers and employers, and the parliamentarians, whose main concern is to win votes, fear an all-out struggle by the rank and file even more than they fear defeat by the ruling class. At the crucial moment they will inevitably betray.

This makes the building of a revolutionary party doubly urgent. Unless a credible alternative, with a substantial base in the working class, *is built in advance* of the general confrontation, the majority of workers will continue to follow their existing leaders — who will lead them to catastrophe as they did in the General Strike of 1926 or in Chile in 1973.

A revolutionary party differs from a reformist party not only in aims and ideas, but also in the nature of its membership, organisation and mode of operation. A reformist party is essentially an electoral machine. Its membership is usually large but passive. Its main jobs are fund-raising and canvassing. This requires neither political education, nor discipline, nor democracy, for no serious action by the party membership is even contemplated. It leads necessarily to the domination of the party by its MPs and its bureaucracy.

A revolutionary party, however, is a combat party. Its membership is smaller (in a non-revolutionary period) but active. Its job is to fight for its political analysis and strategy in all the struggles of the working class, and in so doing win the leadership of the class at rank-and-file level. This requires a high political level, unity in action and real democracy, for the party's politics have to be carried in practice by the members.

Only a party built on these lines can lead the working class in an all-out conflict with the system. Only the working class, informed and strengthened through the leadership of such a party, can make a socialist revolution and create a socialist society.

Suggested reading

THIS READING list is intended to help those who would like to explore the arguments put forward here in greater depth. It is by no means exhaustive, however, and those who would like to go further should consult the 'Books for Socialists' booklist produced by Bookmarks, from which most of the titles that follow have been culled. Copies are available from branch bookstalls of the Socialist Workers Party, or by post from Bookmarks, 265 Seven Sisters Road, Finsbury Park, London N4 2DE.

Chapter 1:
On socialism: **The Communist Manifesto** by Marx and Engels; **The Future Socialist Society** by John Molyneux.
On human nature: chapter two of **How Marxism Works** by Chris Harman.
On workers' power: chapter four of **The Revolutionary Road to Socialism** by Alex Callinicos.

Chapter 2:
On Marxist economics: **Wage Labour and Capital** and **Wages, Price and Profit** by Marx himself; **Man's Worldly Goods** by Leo Huberman.
On economic crisis: **Why the world economy is in crisis** by Peter Green.
On fascism: **Fascism: What it is and how to fight it** by Leon Trotsky.

On revolutionary change: chapter nine of **How Marxism Works** by Chris Harman.

On workers' power: chapter seven of **The Revolutionary Ideas of Karl Marx** by Alex Callinicos.

Chapter 3:

On historical materialism: chapter five of **The Revolutionary Ideas of Karl Marx** by Alex Callinicos.

Chapter 4:

On bourgeois democracy: chapter two of **The Revolutionary Road to Socialism** by Alex Callinicos; **Parliamentary Socialism** by Ralph Miliband.

On the state: **State and Revolution** by Lenin; **Marxists and the State** (Education for Socialists no. 3).

Chapter 5:

On war: **Socialism and War** by Lenin; chapter thirteen of **How Marxism Works** by Chris Harman.

On terrorism: **Against Individual Terrorism** by Leon Trotsky.

On the family: **Women and the struggle for Socialism** by Norah Carlin; chapters thirteen and fourteen of **Class struggle and women's liberation** by Tony Cliff.

Chapter 6:

On internationalism: chapter seven of **The Revolutionary Ideas of Karl Marx** by Alex Callinicos.

On racism: **Racism and Anti-racism** by Peter Alexander.

On liberation movements: **Deflected Permanent Revolution** by Tony Cliff; **South Africa: The Road to Revolution** by Alex Callinicos.

On Ireland: **Ireland's Permanent Revolution** by Chris Bambery; **Labour in Irish History** by James Connolly.

On Russia and Eastern Europe: **Russia: How the revolution was lost** by Alan Gibbons; **Russia: From workers' state to state capitalism** by Peter Binns, Tony Cliff and Chris Harman.

On Stalinism: chapter seven of **What is the real Marxist tradition?** by John Molyneux.

Chapter 7:
On reformism: chapter two of **The Revolutionary Road to Socialism** by Alex Callinicos; **The Labour Party: Myth and Reality** by Duncan Hallas; **Bailing out the System** by Ian Birchall.
On trade unions: chapter three of **The Revolutionary Road to Socialism** by Alex Callinicos; **Marxism and Trade Union Struggle: The General Strike of 1926** by Tony Cliff and Donny Gluckstein; **The Mass Strike** by Rosa Luxemburg.
On the revolutionary party: **Party and Class** by Chris Harman; **Russia: The making of the Revolution** by Steve Wright; **Lenin 1893-1914: Building the Party** by Tony Cliff.

These and many more publications are available from bookshops and local branches of the socialist organisations listed at the front of this book, or by post from:

- **Bookmarks**, 265 Seven Sisters Road, London N4 2DE, England.
- **Bookmarks**, PO Box 16085, Chicago, Illinois 60616, USA.
- **Bookmarks**, GPO Box 1473N, Melbourne 3001, Australia.

Bookmarks bookshop in London also runs a large socialist mail order service. We have stocks of books and pamphlets from many publishers on socialism, internationalism, trade union struggle, women's issues, economics, the Marxist classics, working-class history and much, much more. We're willing to send books anywhere in the world. Write for our latest booklists to:
BOOKMARKS, 265 Seven Sisters Road, Finsbury Park, London N4 2DE, England.